Money

Guid

Planning Your Finances

OTHER TITLES IN THIS SERIES INCLUDE

Moneywise Guide to Your Pension

Moneywise Guide to Tax

Moneywise Guide to Investing in the Stockmarket

Moneywise

Guide to Planning your Finances

Isabel Berwick & Caroline Laws

Moneywise

RD Publications Ltd · London

in association with

Prentice Hall Europe

London New York Toronto Sydney Tokyo Singapore Madrid
Mexico City Munich Paris

First published 1998 by
Prentice Hall Europe
Campus 400, Maylands Avenue
Hemel Hempstead
Hertfordshire HP2 7EZ
A division of
Simon & Schuster International Group

Editorial:
Brown Packaging Books Ltd
Bradley's Close
74–77 White Lion Street
London N1 9PF

Design:
Kingfisher Design, London N2 9NR

Printed and bound in Great Britain by:
T.J. International Ltd, Padstow

Library of Congress Cataloging-in-Publication Data

Available from the publisher

British Library Cataloguing in Publication Data

A Catalogue record for this book is available from the British Library

ISBN: 0-13-911041-0

1 2 3 4 5 03 01 00 99 98

Contents

About the Moneywise Ask the Professionals panel...

Throughout this book you will find comments and explanations from members of the *Moneywise* Ask the Professionals panel. The members are authorised professional advisers specialising in different areas of financial planning who answer *Moneywise* readers' letters every month. The panel aims to answer any financial queries. The service is free and using it puts you under no obligation whatsoever.

For advice write to:
'Ask the Professionals'
Moneywise
11 Westferry Circus
Canary Wharf
London E14 4HE

Janet Adam is a tax partner at chartered accountants BDO Stoy Hayward, based in Manchester

Walter Avrili is operations director at independent mortgage advisers John Charcol in London

Brian Dennehy is an independent financial adviser and managing director of Dennehy, Weller & Co in Kent

Kean Seager is an independent financial adviser and managing director of Whitechurch Securities in Bristol

Keith Sanham is an independent financial adviser at Fairmount Trust Plc, based in Leatherhead, Surrey

Rebekah Kearey is an independent financial adviser and a partner at Roundhill Financial Management in Brighton

Preface

You've just got past the biggest difficulty most people face with their finances. You've got past page 1 – and you're still reading. With most financial literature, that's unusual. Fear, fatigue or frustration would normally have set in by now – caused by figures, jargon, cf paragraph C sub-section three ... and more figures. That's why most financial books go unread, why most bank statements go unopened ... why most self-assessment tax-returns go back late.

But money doesn't have to be that difficult. If you flick through some of these pages, you'll be looking at flowcharts that show your financial choices in simple terms. And with a *Moneywise* publication, that's not unusual. *Moneywise* has always set out to make money make sense – key facts and figures, plain English, clear headings and action points. That's why *Moneywise* is Britain's best-read personal finance magazine ... and probably why you opened this book.

And now that you've started, you'll find it gets easier. As you read more pages of these *Moneywise* guides, you'll get to know more about financial planning, pensions, tax and stockmarket investments. You'll find that this knowedge really does give you power. You'll know what to ask, what to look for and what to expect when you deal with financial companies. You may start by following our action points but go on to work out your own!

All the action points and flowcharts in our guides have been put together with this aim in mind. We asked leading independent financial advisers (IFAs) and *Moneywise*'s award-winning financial journalists to provide you with up-to-date practical advice – not textbook tax book theory.

It's all just over the page. So get past this preface and get to the advice you need. But if you're still standing in the bookshop reading this, go via the cash desk – you'll find this is an investment that will really pay off.

Matthew Vincent
Editor
Moneywise

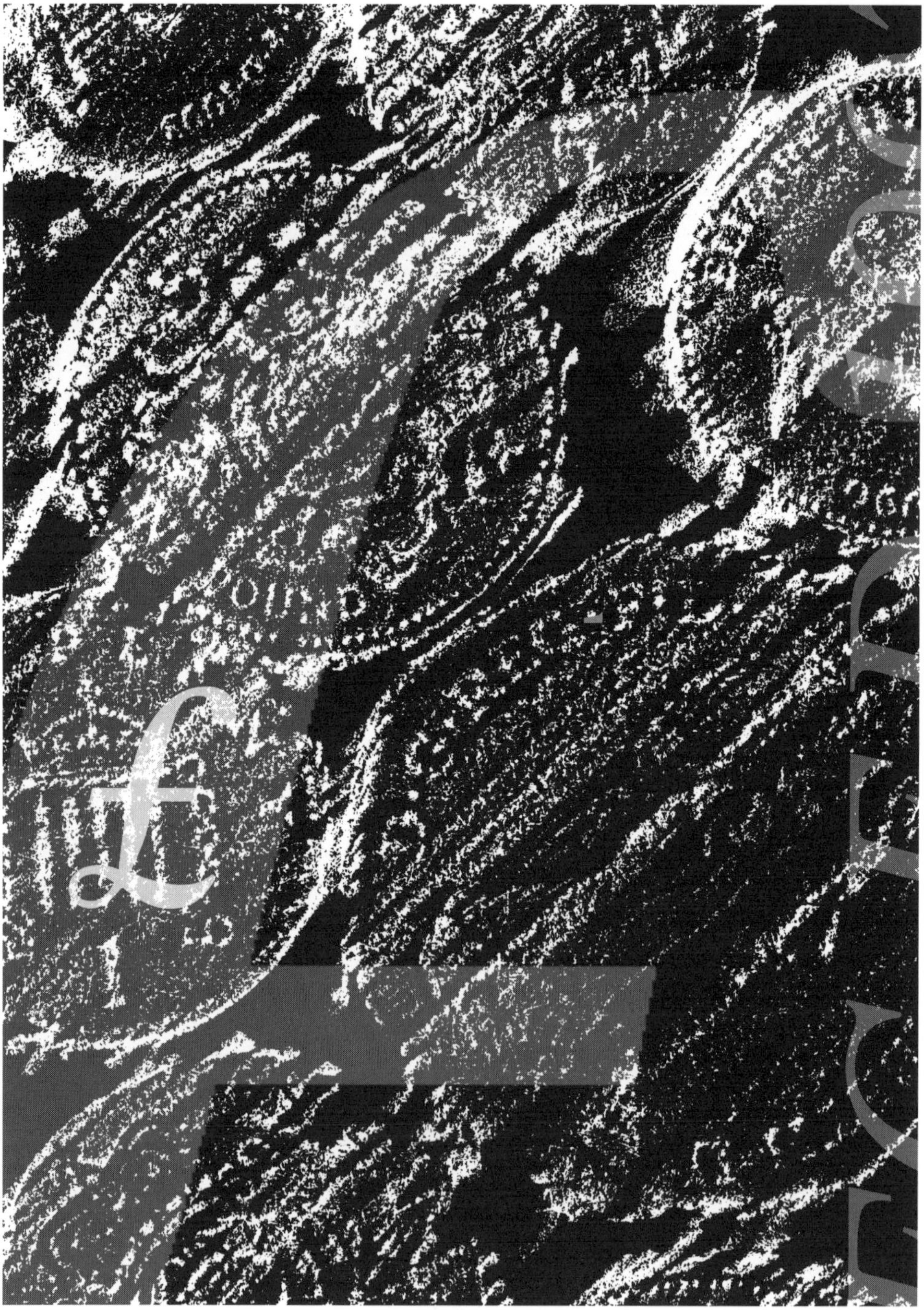

1

Why do you need to plan your finances?

If you're like most people, you probably don't take that much interest in your finances. So long as you've got enough money to pay your mortgage or rent, and you can pay off some or all of your credit card and other regular bills every month, you think you're OK. But the truth is, you're not.

It's up to you to make structured plans to protect your financial future and that of your family.

At *Moneywise* magazine, we hear from thousands of readers every year who know they ought to be doing something about financial planning but are so daunted by the vast amount of advertising and promotional bumf they see that they don't know where to begin. Lots of them end up going to the bank and asking their adviser to help out. Our first tip is right there: never go to the bank as your sole source of financial advice. They've got the bank's profits at heart, not your best interest. They can only sell you the bank's own products – most of which will be more expensive than average.

We want this book to be practical and easy-to-read. Our aim is to make financial planning as easy to understand – and act on – as possible. Let us know what you think of it. Of course tax, pensions and investments are (let's face it) complicated and boring but we've tried to make everything as clear as we possibly can: we've cut through the jargon and highlighted the important points that can make a difference.

Just by buying this book you've made an important decision to face the world of personal financial planning. Gone are the days when you joined a company, worked for it for life, and retired on a decent company pension plus a state pension. The reason we wrote this book is to give some guidance on how you can win a better deal financially in a world where our individual relationships with the welfare system and our employers have changed radically.

This book isn't intended to scare you. We want it to appeal to everyone – from people who aren't sure what they ought to be doing with their money to those who already have a clear understanding of finance issues but who want some more detailed advice.

We recommend that anyone taking their financial planning seriously should consult an independent financial adviser (see Chapter 12), but before you do, you need to have a good idea about what you want and how you would prefer to achieve your aims. By buying ths book, you've already taken the first, important step.

Start right here: use the flowcharts to find out what your financial priorities should be at your age, and where to find more information on the relevant subjects later in the book.

If the idea of reading a whole book on personal finance makes you feel ready to sleep, remember this. It's our biggest tip and the key to all financial planning: the earlier you start to save, the easier it will be for you later. That doesn't mean that anyone who's in their forties or fifties has missed the boat – far from it. A few hours spent studying this book and acting on its recommendations should set you up for the rest of your life, regardless of how old you are now.

Your twenties

Are you married?

Yes

- Make sure you claim married couple's allowance (see Chapter 4).
- Tell insurers you are married – it might get you lower premiums.
- Arrange insurance for you and your spouse. Your first priority should be life cover (see Chapter 6).
- Other things to think about include sickness insurance. You can choose to have a regular income or a lump sum if one of you fell seriously ill and couldn't work (see Chapter 6).

No

- If you have a mortgage, you should make sure the debt would be covered if you were to die (see Chapter 5).
- Think about insuring your salary, which will protect you if you fall seriously ill (see Chapter 6).

Do you have any savings?

Yes

- Build up an emergency fund in an easy access bank or building society account.
- If you have that, and won't need money for a deposit on a house, for example, think about moving some money into more long-term investments. Five-year tax-free savings accounts (TESSAs) or a PEP might suit you (see Chapter 9).

No

- Start saving what you can, but try to pay off your debts first. See Chapter 2 for more on debt.
- When you do start saving, choose an account with a decent rate of interest and easy access. See Chapter 9 for more on building societies.

Do you pay into a pension?

Yes

- If you are in a company scheme, you are in an excellent position. The best type pay out two-thirds of your final salary on retirement.
- Keep paying into any personal pension scheme you are already a member of. The government is planning big changes to the pension system, but you shouldn't stop your contributions in the meantime (see Chapter 7).

No

- If you haven't started paying into a pension and haven't got the chance to pay into a company-run scheme, then it may be worth hanging on to see what the government plans. Your twenties may be unsettled workwise and you should build up savings somewhere in the meantime (see Chapter 8).

Then (both paths):

- Try to save at least 10% of the value of the house you want to buy as a deposit. This will make your mortgage a lot cheaper (see Chapter 5).
- Don't buy your first flat when the market is overheated. Many got stuck with homes worth less than their mortgage loan after the last property slump.

Your thirties

Do you have a partner and/or family?

Yes / No

- You should have insurance in place that will pay out in the event that you or your partner dies.
- Think about taking out extra insurance to cover your salaries – if you and a partner both work, sickness insurance which will replace lost income should be a priority (see Chapter 6).
- Save for children in a tax-efficient way. As parents, you have to be very careful which investments you make because you will be taxed on the child's income (see Chapter 10).
- Make a will and sort out what would happen if you were to die (see Chapter 11).
- Claim the right tax allowances (see Chapter 4).

Do you have any money saved up?

Yes / No

- Aim to save £5,000 in an easy access building society account. Once you have this 'cushion' you can think about moving extra money into long-term low-risk investments such as National Savings and TESSAs (see Chapter 9).
- Start to think about retirement planning. Stockmarket investment through PEPs or unit and investment trusts is a good place to make your money work in the long term (see Chapter 9).
- If you want your children to go to private school, or are thinking ahead to college fees, you'll need to put some money away to fund that (see Chapter 10).

Do you have a pension?

Yes / No

- If you have a personal pension you can put more in after the age of 35: you can increase your contributions from 17.5% to a maximum of 20% of your earnings (see Chapter 7).
- Check that your pension, of whatever type, is on course to deliver you a decent pension. Ask the company pensions officer or your personal pensions provider for projections. Think about making extra contributions through AVCs or FSAVCs. (see Chapter 7).

Are you a higher-rate taxpayer?

Yes / No

- Make the most of tax-free investments (see Chapter 9) and switch some of your investments into your spouse's name if he or she doesn't pay tax or pays at a lower rate.

•If you're single, make sure you take out insurance which would cover all your costs if you were off work sick for a long period (see Chapter 6).
•Divorce is expensive. An endowment policy can often be sold (see Chapter 9). Take preventative measures by keeping life policies and some investments separate (see Chapters 6 and 9).

•Start saving. You need to build up several thousand pounds as an emergency fund in a bank or building society account (see Chapter 8).
•Don't go for fancy stockmarket money-making schemes before you have the basic 'cushion' in place.

•Act now if you don't have a pension. Delaying any longer will be expensive. If your company doesn't offer a scheme, see an independent financial adviser to discuss your options. If you want to wait and see what the government says about pensions, make sure you are contributing to a savings scheme which goes for maximum capital growth (see Chapter 7).

•PEPs aren't so attractive to people who aren't paying 40% tax, but you'll save on paperwork and they are a useful planning tool as long as you don't pay extra for having a PEP wrapper on a unit or investment trust. Other tax-efficient investments, such as TESSAs, are just as attractive to lower-rate as to higher-rate taxpayers (see Chapter 9).

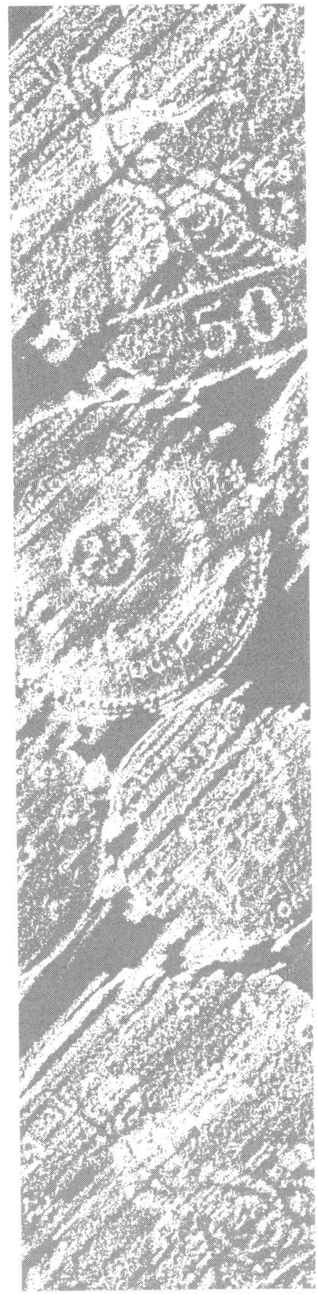

Your forties

Are your savings all in the building society?

Yes No

•Now's the time to think about branching out – you need to make your money grow as fast as possible as you approach retirement. Leave several thousand in the building society but think about other investments. National Savings offer a range for cautious investors and gilts (government bonds) are quite attractive investments. Think about stockmarket investment as a way of boosting capital as well as getting interest on your savings. It isn't all high risk (see Chapter 9).

Are you worried about ill health or losing your job?

Yes No

•You may already have taken out critical illness and income replacement cover to protect your family's lifestyle in case of sickness. Payouts from these plans are tax-free. Act in your early forties if you want to benefit at a reasonable cost (see Chapter 5 for more on these plans).
•You should already have life insurance – perhaps you should think about extra policies. You can set up a policy so that your children will benefit after your death and use the lump sum to pay off any inheritance tax, for example (see Chapter 11).
•Redundancy is a big threat to older workers. Think about measures to reduce outgoings, such as paying off some of the mortgage (see Chapter 2).
•Private medical insurance is expensive. You could keep costs down by choosing a policy which makes you pay an excess, or which only operates when waiting lists are long (see Chapter 5).

Is your pension on course?

Yes No

•Even if you're happy with the way the fund is being run, there may be room for extra contributions. Check the maximum limits on investment and try to put in as much as you can (see Chapter 7).

- Check that you have a balanced mix of investments (see Chapter 8 for investments you may not have heard of, such as guaranteed stockmarket bonds and offshore accounts). Plus, are your stockmarket funds performing well? You may need to change some of your plans (see Chapter 10).
- You can still afford to go for aggressive growth through, for example, emerging markets investments or buying shares in small and unquoted companies. But don't invest anything you can't afford to lose in this way (see Chapter 8 for more on high-risk investments).

- Even if you are on your own, and have no commitments, you still need to make provision to pay off debts if you were to die. Make a will, for starters, and make sure you have some insurance in place that will pay off your mortgage if you die (see Chapter 11).
- If you don't have a partner you are even more vulnerable to redundancy and ill-health, slashing your income. Make sure you have a good savings 'cushion' and consider taking out an income replacement policy (see Chapter 8).

- Have you been mis-sold a poor pension? If you were in an occupational pension scheme and were sold a personal pension in the late 80s and early 90s, make sure your case gets reviewed. You may be due for compensation (see Chapter 7).
- Consider putting in extra money through AVC or FSAVC contributions (see Chapter 7).
- If you're a woman who took years off work through a career break, now's the time to make up lost pension contributions. Put in as much as you can if you're back at work; save for retirement in other ways if you're not (see Chapter 7).
- Divorced women will soon be able to take account of a husband's pension scheme when they divide up their assets (see Chapter 7 for more about divorce and pensions).

Your fifties

Have you paid off the mortgage?

Yes:

•If you've paid off early, it may be worth getting some extra life insurance or seeing whether you can convert a term assurance policy into a whole of life scheme (see Chapter 6).

Do you have elderly parents?

Yes:

•There's little state help for your parents if they need to go into a retirement or nursing home, or even if they just need extra help to make life easier in their own home. There are several options, including taking out an immediate long-term care policy, releasing capital in your parents' home through a home income plan, or a cash plan, which will help pay for the cost of home help (see Chapter 8).
•You should also check that your parents are getting all the state benefits they are entitled to.

Are your retirement plans finalised?

Yes:

•If you plan to retire at 55 or 60 you'll need to be absolutely determined to put as much away as possible during the run-up to retirement (see Chapter 7). And bear in mind that your plans may be upset by sudden illness or redundancy.

Are you giving financial help to children or grand-children?

Yes:

•Make sure you are aware of how much you can give under inheritance tax laws (see Chapters 4 and 11).
•If you are thinking of giving a deposit for a house or a loan to a child, make sure you are clear about whether it's a gift or a loan.
•Investing for grandchildren should be as tax-efficient as possible. Only set up a friendly society children's bond scheme, for example, if you can keep it going for at least ten years (see Chapter 10 for ideas on the best ways to give money to children).

No

•If you're thinking about paying off the mortgage early, your main consideration should be whether you're getting a better return on your investments than the amount you're paying in interest on the loan (see Chapter 5 for more on whether or not to pay off).
•Consider switching to a better mortgage deal. If you want to pay off some of the mortgage but want access to your money in an emergency, a flexible mortgage deal might suit you (see Chapter 5).

•Even if your parents are dead, you may want to think about how you'll finance your own old age. Retirement can last 25 or 30 years. There are several long-term care insurance policies around (see Chapter 6). You may do better to save extra money in your retirement fund and see what the government does to help people fund care costs.
•Taking out a cash plan for yourself now costs little and offers excellent benefits (see Chapter 6).

•If you've had several jobs and paid into several schemes, you need to collect all the documents together and get an expert to help you sort out your pension (see Chapter 12 for how to find a well-qualified adviser).
•You can put up to 15% of your salary in total into an employers pension scheme, AVCs or FSAVCs (see Chapter 7). With a personal pension, you can put in up to 30% of your earnings between the ages of 51 and 55. From 56 to 60 the limit is 35% (see Chapter 7 for more on personal pensions).
•Your investments may need fine-tuning. Move from boosting growth to maintaining income, and take money out of risky funds. Your PEP allowance could be used for corporate bond PEPs (see Chapter 9), aimed at a steady income stream rather than growth.

•Even if you're not making regular payments to relatives, you should have made a will by now so that your estate can be divided according to your wishes and not according to the laws of intestacy (see Chapter 11).

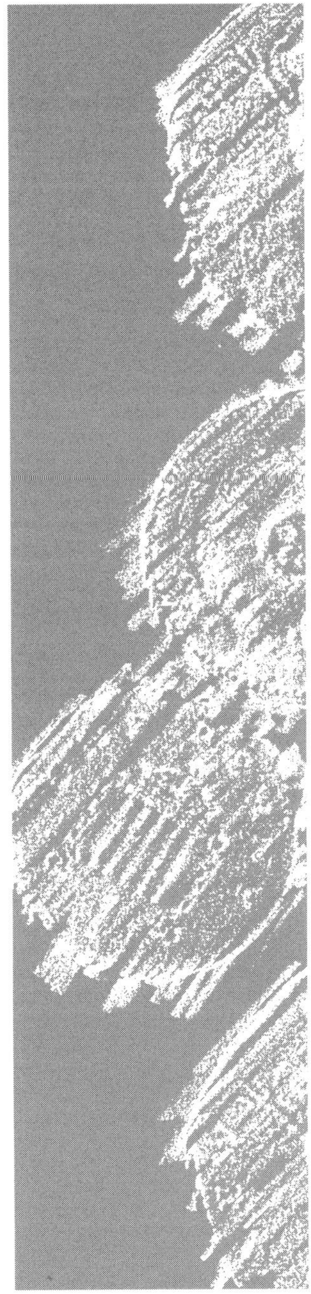

Your sixties and retirement years

Do you need to boost your income in retirement?

Yes →

•If you're still working, make sure you make the most of your pension scheme (see Chapter 7 for how to make additional payments as you approach retirement).
•Check that you've got details of all the pension schemes you've contributed to in your working life and get an adviser to sort out how much you'll get from each of them (see Chapter 12 for how to find an adviser).
•Check that all your investments are on course and make sure you have switched out of high-risk investments (see Chapter 9).

No →

Do you know what to do with your pension when you retire?

Yes →

•Occupational pensions will pay you a lump sum plus an annual income. Also check that you'll get all the state pension benefits you're entitled to (see Chapter 7).
•If you have a personal pension you may already have explored what sort of annuity you can buy with your pension fund. Don't forget the new option to defer taking the bulk of your personal pension money as an annuity – you can leave it until you are 75 and rely on investment income (see Chapter 7 for more on deferred annuities).

No →

Are you facing paying medical and long-term care bills?

Yes →

•Look into the idea of releasing some capital from your home through a safe home income plan (SHIP) (see Chapter 10).
•A high-income investment plan may be enough to buy you some care in your home (see Chapter 6). These plans offer a steady income but your capital may be eroded.
•Long-term care insurance plans have yet to gain much popularity, but they are available as either immediate annuities, bought with a lump sum, or as straight insurance policies (see Chapter 6).
•Sickness can strike suddenly: if you or your spouse is diagnosed with a terminal illness you can often cash in a whole life insurance policy. This will release funds to make your last months or years easier (see Chapter 6 for more on this).

No →

Have you planned how your estate will be passed on to your heirs?

Yes →

•Even if you've made a will, make sure it's up to date. You may not realise how much your estate is worth – if you have more than £215,000 worth of assets your heirs will have to pay inheritance tax (see Chapter 11).

No →

•Check that you are doing all you can to make the most of the inheritance tax rules (see Chapter 3). You might also consider using a trust as a protective home for some of your assets (see Chapter 11).

•If you have a personal pension your pension fund rolls up into a lump sum and you have to use it to buy an annual income, known as an annuity (see Chapter 7 for more on this). You don't have to buy it from the company which sold you the pension.

•Even if you are in good health, it's worth taking some measures to protect you against financial hardship when you are extremely old and frail. Take out a cashplan while you still can (see Chapter 6).

•Make sure you are topped up with life insurance: this can be hard to buy when you are in poor health (see Chapter 6).

•Now's the time to get some expert advice on your will and inheritance tax, especially if you have been married more than once, have children from different relationships, or just have a complicated financial life (see Chapter 11 for what to do).

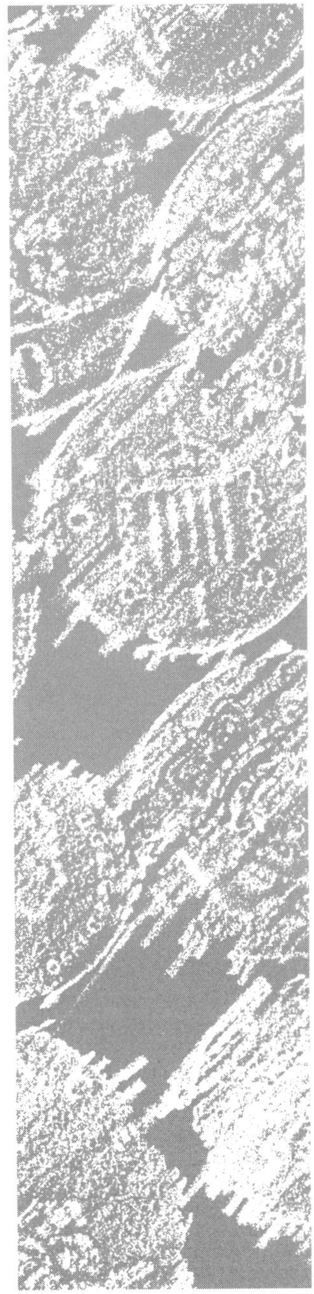

2

Money basics

Before you get down to the serious business of making significant or long-term financial planning decisions, you need to make sure the basics are organised. If you're sure you've got all the basics sewn up – the right bank account and the right credit card, for example – you can go straight to the next chapter.

In this chapter we help you:

- *Establish your current financial position and improve your cash flow.*
- *Get the best from your bank.*
- *Review your credit cards.*
- *Never worry about a bill again.*

Establish your position

MANY OF US have no idea where all the money goes. When you're young, you're paying off student debts or perhaps struggling to juggle a low salary and high rent. Once you've saddled yourself with a mortgage, a car and a family, you're a fully fledged consumer, and it's hard to take a step back and remember that you have to make plans for tomorrow as well as making a living today.

> **TIP**
> Set up a filing system for all your financial and personal affairs. Get a sturdy a–z file and put in all your bills, receipts, insurance documents and bank statements. Sort it out and throw away the old bills when you review your finances every year.

Whatever stage you're at in life, you need to work out what your current money position is before you can replan your finances. In short, what are you worth? It's a chore to sort out all your assets and liabilities but when you've done it once it won't be so painful next time. And there will be a next time – sitting down to review your finances should be an annual affair, not a once-in-a-lifetime desperation measure.

Start by buying a small notebook and carrying it everywhere, noting down

YOU AND YOUR FINANCES WORKSHEET

When you have kept a record of your outgoings for a month, fill in this chart.

INCOME	
Salary	
Pay from other work	
Income from relatives, etc	
Income from investments (eg share dividends, interest on savings)	
Other payments (eg grants, pensions, benefits)	
TOTAL	

OUTGOINGS	
Mortgage or rent	
Loans (car, student, home improvement loan, etc)	
Council Tax and utility bills	
Car expenses (petrol, insurance, repairs)	
Buildings and contents insurance	
Life insurance	
Other personal insurance (eg medical, income replacement)	
Home expenses (eg furnishing, computers, garden equipment)	
Dental/opticians' expenses	
Medical/care expenses	
Credit card repayments and interest	
Tax payments	
Regular savings plans	
Childcare/school and university fees	
Bank charges	
Food bills	
Holidays	
Entertainment (cinema, theatre, eating out, pubs, etc)	
Presents	
Personal care (hairdressers, chemists)	
Membership fees	
Donations to charity	
Clothes	
Magazines, newspapers, books	
Pets and vets' bills	
Hobbies	
Other expenses	
TOTAL	

The important figures: Total monthly income

minus total outgoings

equals MONTHLY SHORTFALL/SURPLUS

Independent financial adviser and *Moneywise* Ask The Professionals panellist Brian Dennehy says:

"Personal loans are relatively cheap. If you have a number of expensive debts (credit cards!), get a personal loan to pay them off and tear up all your credit cards. With Switch-type facilities available credit cards are unnecessary for most people."

everything you spend for a month. If you're working, start on the day your salary cheque is paid into your bank account. When you've finished, break down all the spending into different categories and fill in your checklist (see over). You'll be amazed by how much you spend on non-essentials that you could cut out altogether. A coffee bought on the way to work every day might cost £1 a day. Cut it out and you've saved more than £200 a year without trying.

Obviously some of your expenses won't occur every month. But once you've got your filing system going you can work out how much they average over a year, and break that down to monthly averages. For example, if you go to a dentist twice a year and the treatment over the past year has cost a total of £80, that's a rather more reasonable £6·67 a month.

What to do next

If you have a monthly shortfall: Make sure there isn't some big item that has skewed your finances. If not, you are probably spending more than you earn each month and you may well end up with a serious problem. Debt isn't a problem in itself. Managed debt allows you to borrow enough to meet pressing needs when you haven't got the capital to pay from savings – when buying a car, for example. Many of us have loans and leave a balance on our credit card at the end of the month.

So how can you tell if you have an embryonic debt problem? Warning signs include: difficulty meeting your monthly repayments on loans; not making in-roads into credit card bills – and maybe even letting them grow; and hardly ever being in credit at the bank, except perhaps for a week after payday.

Tip
If you're concerned about your debt, add up all the money you owe. Don't include your mortgage. If the total is more than about 20% of your annual pay, after tax, then you need to work hard to reduce it.

If you have already progressed beyond the early warning signs of debt then you, and all those around you, probably know what's going on. You need to get professional advice. Many of those who end up needing help are people with good jobs who have simply over-committed themselves to buy a better lifestyle for their families. A sudden drop in income – from redundancy, illness or divorce – can mean that the debt suddenly becomes hard to manage.

Speak to all the organisations and people to whom you owe money. The worst possible reaction is to hide all the envelopes unopened. You don't want to end up in court for non-payment of debt, as this will make it very hard for you to get credit in future. Creditors to whom you owe money can pursue you for six years after the last date they tried to contact you.

Take all the information you have about your finances along to a money adviser who is attached to a Citizens Advice Bureau (the local branch will be in the phone book). Alternatively, call National Debtline. Their advisers will be able to give advice over the phone, and this might be the right first step if you are trying to keep your money worries to yourself. The phone number is 0645 500511. A debt adviser is trained to take an overview of your problems and work with you and your creditors to put a realistic repayment plan in place. Many credit card companies and financial firms will agree to a small regular payment once they have been told about your changed circumstances.

It might take years to get your finances back in order – and until you do that, you can't start to work towards a more secure future. Don't let it get to that. And don't, ever, take out a loan to pay off all your other loans. Many loan companies, especially those which target less-well-off people and collect repayments door-to-door, charge rip-off rates of interest. Their customers are often people who are already in debt who are encouraged to take out a single loan to get all their other creditors off their backs. You could end up with an interest rate of several hundred per cent. Steer well clear.

TIP
You can always sell some of your assets to generate some cash. That doesn't have to mean selling the TV: car boot sales are hugely popular. A pitch costs less than £10 and you can make £100 or more in a morning.

If you have a surplus each month: Even if your finances look healthy there'll be room for improvement. There's no point in trying to get your financial priorities sorted out until you have reorganised your basic spending patterns and worked out how much money you really have to spare. Check all your outgoings – especially your entertainment budget. Aim to cut them by about 10%. Once you have sorted out your cashflow, you need to put in place the basic building blocks for your financial future. Central to that is your relationship with the people who look after your money. Start with the bank.

Get the best from your bank

THINK BACK TO WHY you opened your first bank account with one particular bank. Was it the fact that your parents banked there? Was it the only branch near your home? Or was it the bank that offered the best bribe when you first started at college?

No wonder banks spend millions wooing schoolchildren and students. Once you've decided on a bank, you're unlikely to move your current account. Ever. And once you're hooked in with a bank you represent a goldmine of potential money-making opportunities. All the big banks – with the exception of the Co-operative Bank, which gives independent advice – only sell a range of their own financial products, including mortgages and pensions.

It's time to work out whether your bank is still working for you. Now you're intimate with your own finances, you'll have an idea of what kind of customer you are. Banks are constantly trying to retune their products to get the most money from their customers. Follow this checklist to work out whether you should shop around for a better deal.

ALWAYS IN CREDIT?

- If you keep a balance on your current account then you must make sure it's paying you interest. This is likely to be paltry – little more than 1% – but every little helps.
- You're probably being bombarded with offers from your bank to sign up for new-style current accounts, which come with all sorts of bells and whistles – free life insurance, lower-cost overdrafts, a magazine, and so on – but it all comes at a price, of up

to £8 a month. We're sceptical about these accounts. It's just not worth it unless you really feel that you'll get good value from the 'perks'.

Need an occasional overdraft?

- You should definitely be getting interest on your current account but make sure that the bank doesn't overcompensate with punitive charges for people who go overdrawn.
- Find a bank which offers interest-free overdrafts for small amounts (usually up to £100 or £250).

Usually overdrawn?

Steer clear of the big banks and see what the ex-building societies and the telephone bank, First Direct, have to offer. They may be happy to take you on even if you have an overdraft. If you are being charged a monthly fee as well as interest on your overdraft then you'll find a better deal elsewhere.

If you are considered a poor credit risk – perhaps you've had problems meeting a loan in the past, for example – you're stuck with your bank as you are unlikely to be welcomed with open arms anywhere else.

Check your bank statements

Barclays Bank says that four in ten of us never look at our bank statements. It's easy to see why an evening with your cheque stubs, debit card slips and a bank statement might be considered less than exciting. But the upside is that you might spot a mistake – and you can ask the bank to refund you for it, with compensation. They can only say no – and if they do, you can take your business elsewhere. If you find something that has been wrongly credited to your account – a cheque intended for someone with the same name, for example – it's your duty to tell the bank. If you spend the money the bank has the right to ask you to pay it back.

Tip

The big four high street banks rarely win top marks for service from customers. Smaller banks and the ex-building societies want to get a bigger slice of current account business and are prepared to offer better deals. See what they have to offer if you are thinking of swapping.

Telephone banking is also a good bet as the costs are lower and you'll get a favourable charging structure. The downside is that people who like to do their banking in person will miss the convenience of a huge branch network.

Make sure all your direct debits and standing orders are going through smoothly. At *Moneywise* magazine we've heard from several readers who assumed that endowment policy payments were being made from their accounts, only to find after several years that the policy had never been set up properly, or that the payments were actually going into someone else's bank account! You may find yourself having to start all over again with a new policy.

MONEY BASICS

Review your credit cards

MOST OF US carry a credit card and use it to spread the cost of major purchases. In the last few years there's been a revolution in the way that we use plastic, and the competition for customers is intense. You can get a credit card which earns you points off your gas bill, money off a new car, or even a cash-back arrangement.

Be sure that you know the difference between a credit card and a charge card. A credit card offers you exactly that – a credit facility allowing you to spend up to your agreed limit on your Visa, Mastercard or American Express account. You don't have to pay it all off each month. Whereas with a charge card – like the original American Express card, some Gold Cards, and Diners Club – you have to pay off the bill each month. In return you get perks such as lost luggage insurance, medical insurance, and travel discounts.

> **TIP**
> You can get a free credit card if you pay off your bill every month.

Finding the right credit card to suit you depends on two things: your willingness to swap from your existing card issuer, and how you actually use the card. Different cards suit different spending patterns. Don't be worried about taking out a card with an issuer you haven't heard of. All card issuers have to be licensed. And remember – you're borrowing from them, so they can't run off with your money! There are several American card issuers advertising in the UK now, and they all offer low interest rates because they have low overheads – meaning there's no branch network to support and they have offices set up in cheaper parts of the country.

WHAT SORT OF A CONSUMER ARE YOU?

You always pay off the bill each month: The credit card issuers hate your sort, which is why most of the main high street banks started charging annual fees of £10 or £12. They decided they weren't making enough money because people who pay off each month don't run up interest charges. On most credit cards you get up to 56 days' grace before you are charged interest on your goods. Unless you collect 'points' for a reward scheme – such as Air Miles – then it's unlikely that a card issued by the high street banks will give you good value for money. They are extremely expensive, costing you up to 10% more annual interest than a cheap credit card. Look for a no-fee card with 56 days' credit and an interest rate below 18%.

You sometimes leave a balance on the card for a month or two: The same advice applies. Get a low-cost, no-frills card.

You always carry debt from one month to the next: There is plenty of choice for this group, who are a dream-come-true for credit card companies. If you pay a £12 annual fee, plus 23% interest, then you are practically funding these people's pensions. Get out of the deal at once. You could halve the cost of your borrowing by switching. There are special cards designed for people who leave a balance. They have low interest rates but the catch is that you don't get an interest-free period, so you'll pay less interest in total, but the interest is charged from the day you buy. The Royal Bank of Scotland and the Co-operative Bank are the leaders in this market.

However, there are better deals about. A no-fee card with 56 days' interest-free credit and a low interest rate will give you the chance to pay off your debts and save money, if you unexpectedly have a lump sum, for example.

Once you've decided what sort of card you want, have a look at the 'best buys' in weekend papers to see what deals are on offer. Check that there isn't a catch:

- Is the interest rate for a limited period only? What will it go up to after the 'hook' has lured you into getting a card?

> Independent financial adviser and *Moneywise* Ask The Professionals panellist Brian Dennehy says:
>
> "APRs help you compare like with like. But if you're considering a range of borrowing options you aren't comparing like with like! Common sense and simple maths are often a better substitute."

What is an APR?

You'll see the term APR quoted all over the place in financial advertising. It stands for annual percentage rate. This is the real amount of interest you'll be charged on a loan, credit card or mortgage on a yearly basis.

You'll notice that the APR will be higher than the headline loan rate. For example, you might see a credit card advertised with a monthly interest rate of 1·65%. Multiplying that by 12 months gets you to 19·8% a year, but the card's APR is 21·7%. That's because an APR also includes all other charges.

The idea of an APR is that it 'levels the playing field' and makes it easier for you to compare different products before you decide.

- Is there a special deal for people who transfer balances from one credit card to another? (It's easy to do this. Your new credit card issuer will send a cheque to the old one to cover your debt – it then gets transferred to the new card.)
- Check the small print. Some advertisements which claim that you can save hundreds of pounds a year by swapping cards are basing their assumptions on a £2,000 balance. If your debts are more modest, the savings will be modest too.

Never worry about a bill again

You're not really in control of your finances if you never remember to pay bills on time. Budgeting across the whole year makes everything much easier. You can set up direct debits for your utility bills, TV licence and council tax. That way, the money comes straight out of your bank account. Keep a close eye on how much is being taken each month or quarter: some people end up with hundreds of pounds-worth of credit on their gas account, for example. If this happens, contact the company and ask for your direct debits to be suspended until the credit is used up. And don't forget to check your bank account to make sure your request has been carried out. If you're uneasy with direct debits, look back over at least a year's worth of bills and work out how much to set aside each month.

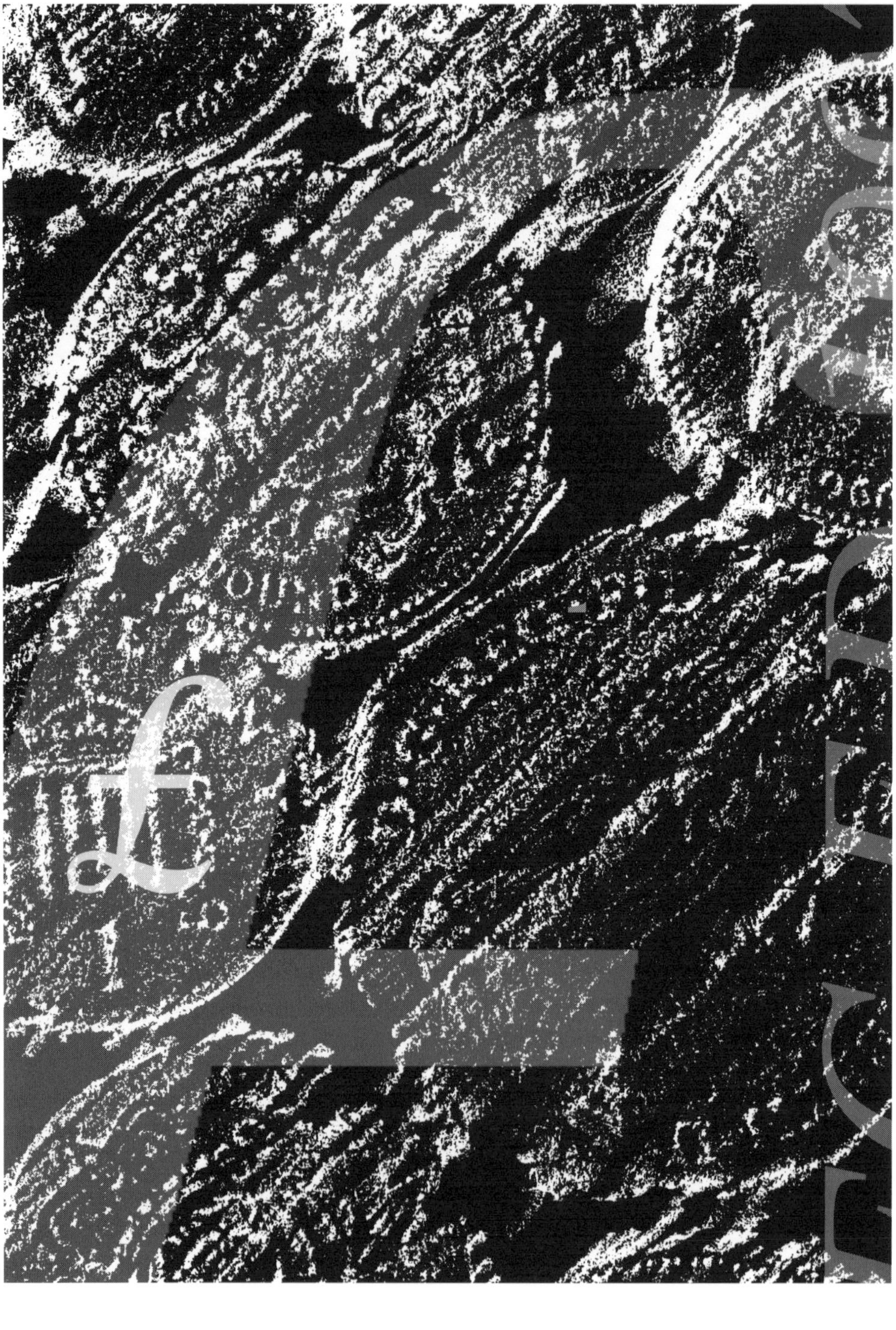

3 Making your plans

The flowcharts in Chapter 1 should have given you an idea of the kinds of financial priorities you should have. In this chapter we look at these plans in more detail.

Most of us have yet to wake up to the fact that the welfare state is changing. The country just can't afford the old 'cradle to grave' health and benefits system that we all know. But it's not all doom. Some things we hold dear do look set to continue – the right to free hospital treatment, for example.

The blurring is at the edges of state provision. Most of us already have to pay for dentists and opticians, and social services in many areas can't provide all the services needed by older and disabled people.

But 1997 has seen a new government and there is a new, more community-minded spirit in the country. A recent survey on social change by the researchers at the Henley Centre found that people believe that the quality of life in Britain will be most improved by promoting the good of the community, rather than the good of the individual. The proportion in favour of the community approach was 70%, against 30% who put individual concerns first. The researchers were asking the same question they'd used in a 1992 survey, which found that 70% of people thought that looking to your own best interests was the best way forward for the good of everyone. (Source: *Swiss Re Life Insurance Report 1997*, page 10.)

This reversal of opinion should ensure that the next few years will see a radical shift in the way we are encouraged to make our financial plans. Pensions, for example, are likely to be given a new direction. The damage done by the personal pensions mis-selling scandal shows how easy it is for cash-hungry businesses to take advantage of people who have little or no understanding of the financial world.

You may want to put your pension plans on hold until we've found out what the government policy will be on pensions. Don't do that – delay causes real problems because your money, quite literally, has less time to work for you and grow in a pension plan. However, you should be aware of what's happening in Parliament and keep your planning relevant and flexible. We'll tell you how to do that in the rest of this chapter.

Whatever happens, you won't lose money in future because you were careful and prudent during the early 1990s. And whatever retirement planning route is chosen by the Labour government, you can be sure that it will ask everyone to pay into personal plans – you can't rely on a state pension alone. The country just can't afford it: by the year 2021 there will be more than 12 million people aged over 65 in the UK. That's nearly 20% of the total population (Source: Help the Aged, 1997).

HOW MUCH TIME HAVE YOU GOT?

You need to work out what your priorities should be and to sort out a rough timescale for future planning. For example, if you are in your forties and have teenage children, the biggest priority might be funding your children's college education. A longer-term goal would be to pay off the mortgage and get your retirement plans in place.

In general, your priorities will depend on how old you are. Your own individual case may be slightly different, but the aim is not to copy our charts, but to use them as a tool to get you thinking about what to put in your own plans. At this stage it doesn't matter too much if you aren't familiar with the best ways to invest money or take out insurance policies to reach your goals. We'll deal with that in other chapters. What's important is to put a framework in place so that you know what you are aiming for.

We've set out our lists of possible financial priorities by age. But read all of them – there's plenty of overlap and something from another section may be relevant to your life and future plans. We've also given an outline of the types of solution available for each planning objective and we've ranked the planning ideas in the order we think they ought to be addressed. Note the ones that apply to you, in order of importance. Then move on to read the relevant chapters to find out how to put your list into practice.

Up to 30: no ties

Save like mad

If you are in your early twenties, starting a savings plan is the first thing you should do when you begin work. Make sure you open an account paying a decent rate of interest, so look in the weekend press and *Moneywise* before you make your choice. Aim to save at least 10% of your take-home pay each month. If you can't manage that, every little helps.

Eventually your savings fund should be big enough to divide into two parts: an emergency fund of perhaps £5,000, left untouched but where you can get easy access to it, and a separate fund for expenses such as a deposit on a house or for buying appliances and furniture.

> **Tip**
> Saving up to pay cash for a big purchase is a good idea, but you should use your credit card to pay in the shop, then pay the bill with your savings. Credit cards give you more protection if something goes wrong or the supplier goes bust.

Put the banking basics in place

Look back to Chapter 2 and make sure that your credit card and banking arrangements aren't costing you some of your precious savings.

Pension planning

Realistically you probably won't start paying into a pension as soon as you start work. People in their twenties may move jobs several times, and many employers don't let under-25s join pension schemes. That doesn't excuse you from adding pension planning to your list of priorities. If you don't join a pension scheme straightaway there are plenty of other ways to put money aside in a retirement fund. As soon as your employment pattern has settled down you'll be able to plan whether to join a company pension or take out a personal scheme.

Insure your possessions

You should do this regardless of whether you share a rented house or have bought your own home. If you are renting, work out how much your possessions would cost to replace – don't forget your clothes as well as TVs and hi-fi equipment. See Chapter 4 for more information about buildings and contents insurance if you are already a homeowner.

Buy a house

Buying a home is a huge commitment so you must take time to be absolutely sure that you understand what you are getting into. Chapter 6 deals with mortgages in some detail. You may remember a recent scandal surrounding the sale of endowment policies to pay off mortgages. An endowment policy can be a good idea, but too many of the people who were sold these schemes in the past didn't really understand what they were buying, and the salespeople took advantage of that – endowments generate lots of commission payments. It's yet another example of how it can pay to be 'in the know' about money.

When you're deciding how much to borrow, most lenders will offer you a loan of up to three times your gross (pre-tax) salary. Some will go higher than that – up to 3·75 times your salary. If you are buying with someone else you can get up to 2·5 times your joint salaries. Don't overstretch yourselves. House prices are rising fast in some parts of the country and in your twenties and thirties you may be on a decent salary with plenty of spare cash. But once you have a family you may find that earning power eroded – a high-earning woman may take a career break, for example – and you don't want to be left struggling to meet monthly repayments.

Up to 45: family ties

Build up your savings

Keep adding to your funds. As you should be looking to leave the money untouched for the long term, it's a good idea to make the most of tax-free investments. These include National Savings Certificates and tax-exempt special savings accounts (TESSAs). To get the tax-free benefits of a TESSA you have to leave the money untouched for five years.

At this stage you should also be thinking of moving some savings into stockmarket-based investments. This is also a long-term commitment, at least five years. Lots of people are wary about taking out any kind of stockmarket investment. But if you want to make your savings work really hard, you're going to have to take some risk. Although your money is safe in the building society or a National Savings account, you won't see any growth in your capital. As inflation goes up over time, your capital value goes down. The low rates of interest paid on savings accounts won't compensate for this. When you invest in shares the value of the shares is likely to go up, plus you get a cash bonus – a dividend – paid out when times are good. Because of the stockmarket's volatility, you need to leave your share investments untouched for several years. If you feel very uncomfortable about shares, there are other stockmarket-based investments which carry a lower-risk profile. Some PEPs, for example, hold fixed-interest funds which buy company bonds and government bonds, known as gilts. These pay higher interest than you'd get from a savings account but there's little (if any) capital growth.

Insure your lives

Life insurance is pretty straightforward. If you die, it pays out a cash sum. When looking at policies you'll find that the words insurance and assurance mean the same thing. Most important, if you have bought a house you need to arrange for the loan to be paid off if you or your partner die. If you don't, the debt will pass into your estate and then your heirs will have to deal with it.

Some employers will arrange a death benefit if you die – this is usually three or four times your gross salary. If you don't have that, or want extra cover, you should consider buying a term assurance policy. As its name suggests, the insurance only covers a fixed term, in this case the repayment period of the mortgage. It will pay off what's left of the loan if you or your partner should die during the repayment period. If you don't die during the 25-year repayment period, you get nothing back. At this stage you also need to work out how much extra insurance you'll need to help your family survive if the main

> Independent financial adviser and *Moneywise* Ask The Professionals panellist Rebekah Kearey says:
>
> "Life insurance produces a lump sum which can be invested to produce income. Family income benefit pays a regular (fixed, rising or decreasing) income for a fixed period on the death of the person insured.
>
> Whichever is most appropriate, it should be written in trust for the beneficiary to avoid potential tax liabilities."

breadwinners die. Add up how much income you need to replace if one or both of you should die.

Protect your family's lifestyle

This is an area where the individual is now expected to plug gaps left by the welfare state. If you fall sick and can't work for months, or even the rest of your life, you could face poverty. The message hasn't really caught on yet, but sickness and disability payments from the state aren't going to get you very far any more. For 1997/98 you'll get £55·70 a week in statutory sick pay. Many employers offer more generous sick pay schemes, so check what cover you have before putting this insurance on your financial planning shopping list.

If you are still off work after 28 weeks, you apply for incapacity benefit. You have to prove you can't do your normal job. If you are successful, you'll get £55.70 a week. Once you've been off work sick for just over a year, you have to prove that you can't do any job at all – and the benefit rate will rise to £62.45 a week. You'll get extra money if you have children. But the long-term benefit is taxable, so if you have enough income to make you a taxpayer you will lose the advantage of the extra few pounds a week.

You can avoid poverty by taking out insurance that will pay out a lump sum if you are diagnosed with a serious illness, or a plan which replaces your income if you're off work sick for some time. One in eight people who are 35 now will suffer a critical illness before they are 60, compared to one in 13 who will die. (Source: Munich Re/Canada Life). The most sobering statistic is that you have a 20% chance of being off work sick for six months or more during your working life. At this stage assume that you want to protect 75% of your income every month. You can't take out insurance to cover your whole salary. Decide whether both partners are going to take insurance.

> Independent financial adviser and *Moneywise* Ask The Professionals panellist Rebekah Kearey says:
>
> "Single people should try hard to fund for both critical illness cover and income replacement. Who else will support them except themselves? If a choice has to be made between the two types of cover, family breadwinners should first consider the size of their existing savings and the cash-flow if the main breadwinner is ill long term. Some families do well by taking critical illness for the breadwinner and income replacement for the partner on a lower income."

Paying for children's education

It costs anything up to £224,000 to bring up a child. If you plan to educate your children in state schools, you still need to set aside money for day-to-day expenses and plan for college costs. The amounts you need to set aside will depend on how many children you have, how old they are when you start saving, and which investment methods you use.

Pension planning

This should be a top priority at any age, but, let's face it, there are many other calls on your money at this time. By this stage you should be putting money into a company or personal pension scheme. You need to find out whether it's likely to be enough. Bear in mind that your pension objective should be to retire on two-thirds of your final salary. Decide how much that's likely to be to give yourself a rough target figure. Remember, you'll be looking at your objectives regularly, so you can make adjustments according to changes in your circumstances.

Coping with divorce

This is increasingly common and financially ruinous, especially for women. If your marriage is in the process of breaking up you must keep a close eye on your finances. Make lists of your joint assets – and remember, if you have bought a home together you are both liable for the mortgage repayments. If one of you decides not to pay up, the other ex-partner will have to pay the whole bill – or face having a huge stain placed on their credit record. Women who have let their husbands or partners look after their finances in the past may suddenly find themselves starting from scratch with lenders and may also find it very difficult to get a credit card, for example.

Tip

Never, ever let one partner do all the financial planning. Even if one of you is a finance fanatic there's no excuse for the other to do nothing. Start by reading the finance pages in the weekend press. The bottom line is that a little financial knowledge could save you a lot of money if you ever split up.

45–55: pre-retirement frenzy

Yet more savings

Middle age brings with it the greater prospect of the occasional lump sum from an inheritance, or redundancy. We'll look at the options for investment later in the book. You may want to pay off the remaining capital outstanding on your mortgage, for example.

Pension planning

See above: now it's getting seriously close and you need to act fast.

Insure your lives

Don't let the insurance slip – this may be the time when your mortgage is paid off, so you may be left without cover.

Protect your income

See above.

Financing care for elderly parents

This is another area where state assistance has all but disappeared. If your parents have more than £16,000 worth of assets, they won't get any state help if one or both have to go into a retirement home or a nursing home. Their house – which may be your inheritance – may also be vulnerable. There are plans afoot to sort out the funding mess, but the Labour government may take several years to formulate a policy and pass the relevant legislation.

In the short term you may need to help out elderly parents who need extra help in the home. That means cash. If there's no immediate need for care but you are planning ahead, there are also insurance plans available for you or your parents. We've included details in the book but think carefully before you take out this insurance – it's expensive and you may never have to call on it.

55–70: early retirement years

EMERGENCY SAVINGS

At this stage you may find it hard to keep saving. If you haven't fully funded your pension you may even eat into some emergency savings. Accept that this might happen but don't let your 'cushion' drop below £5,000, which must be left untouched.

SORT OUT A DECENT ANNUITY

When you retire you can opt for a tax-free lump sum whatever sort of pension you have. If you are a member of a public service pension scheme or a company final-salary scheme your pension will then be paid automatically. If you have any other sort of pension you will need to use the fund you have built up to buy an income for the rest of your life, called an annuity.

A new option, called a drawdown facil ity, lets you take out lump sums but leave most of your fund untouched until you are 75. The big bonus with drawdown is that if you die before you take the annuity, your heirs will get your pension fund. With a normal annuity, they'd get nothing unless you'd bought an income which continues to pay out to the surviving spouse.

> Independent financial adviser and *Moneywise* Ask The Professionals panellist Rebekah Kearey says:
>
> "The best annuity for you won't necessarily be offered by your pension provider and so your fund can be taken to the best annuity provider at the time of your retirement.
>
> Some annuity providers offer enhanced rates for certain pre-existing medical conditions. An independent financial adviser can offer a list of the best rates, and they are also listed in the major finance magazines and on the Internet."

PROTECTING INCOME IF ONE OF YOU IS SICK OR DIES

You need to work out how much income each spouse gets now and how that would be affected if the other died. If there's a shortfall, you'll need to find a way round it, such as setting aside some savings. At this age, life insurance starts to get expensive, so a new policy may not be an option.

If one of you becomes terminally ill, and already has a whole-of-life insurance policy, you can sell it to a non-profit making firm which specialises in this field. You can then use the cash to make the most of the time you have left. Some life offices also allow people with only a few months to live to cash in their policies and take the money.

If you've had critical illness or income replacement policies, they probably ran out when you retired, so you need to work out how you'd cope with serious illness.

Anyone who's been used to private medical insurance will find that it's extremely expensive once they are over 55. If you decide to drop the insurance plan, there are some other options you may want to consider, such as taking out a healthcare cash plan. Some of these plans 'fast track' you by paying for an initial specialist's appointment, and then you can revert to NHS treatment. The plans also pay out cash towards dental and optical costs.

Inheritance tax planning

Start sorting out your estate and make the most of tax breaks. The good news for many people is that they may not have to make too many plans – you can now have an estate worth £215,000 before your heirs will have to pay inheritance tax. That figure includes the value of your home. Do a rough calculation to find out whether your estate is likely to be taxed.

It's worth making the most of tax breaks available for people who are reducing their assets by giving money and gifts to friends and family. For example, you can make tax-exempt gifts to your family and friends of up to £250 each a year. And you can give £5,000 to a child who's getting married. Other cash gifts usually become tax-free if you live for seven years after you hand over the gift. After you die, any tax due is either paid by the people who received the gifts, or it is charged to your estate.

70 plus: late retirement

Keep a savings cushion

Try to keep your savings intact if you can. Of course this can be very hard when you are living on a limited retirement income and have little spare cash for 'extras'. Use your judgement – if you want to enjoy yourself by dipping into savings, do so. After all, it's your money and you should make it work for you. It's all too easy to forget that your retirement is the 'rainy day' you've been saving for all your life.

Invest money for income

You may need to eat into some of your cash reserve and invest the money to generate an income if your needs change – for example, if you need to pay for care costs. At this stage in life, raising cash against the value of your home may also be an option. If you own your home outright, a home income plan will free some cash to provide you with an annual income. In effect, you'll be taking out a new mortgage on part of the value of your house. You don't have to repay the loan in your lifetime – it can be paid back to the home income company when the house is sold after your death.

Protecting income after the death of one partner

Keep checking on your insurance situation. By now, any endowment policies you have are likely to have matured, giving you a lump sum which can be invested. If you have a spouse who is frail or doesn't understand finance, make sure that you have appointed someone you can trust to safeguard his or her financial position after your death. A trusted relative or solicitor appointed as your executor should take on the role.

Inheritance tax planning

Keep your will up-to-date. As time goes on, new grandchildren and great-grandchildren may need to be added into your instructions. If your estate is likely to attract a tax charge, make sure you are doing all you can to offset this – without depriving yourself of the funds you need for a comfortable retirement.

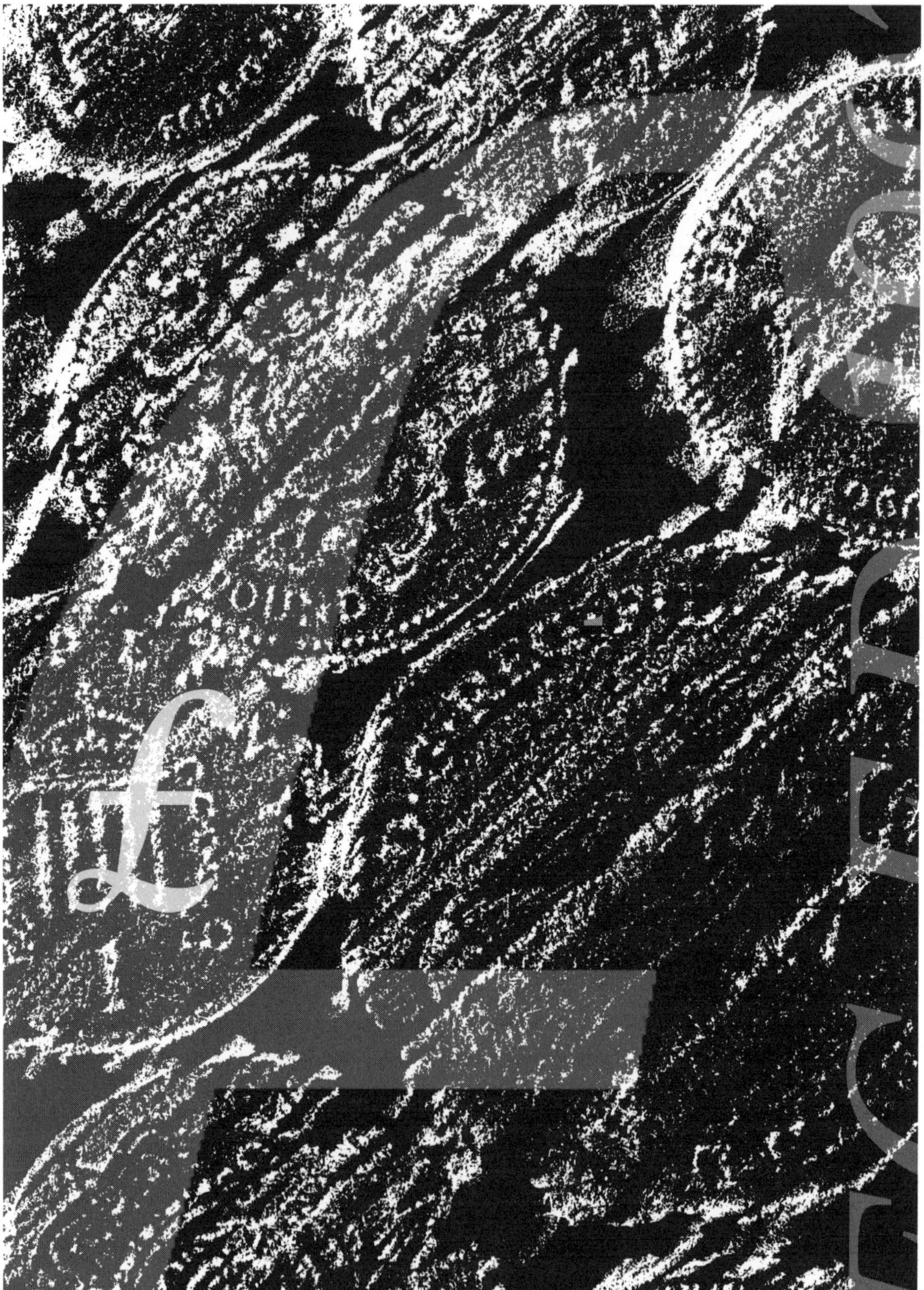

4 Tax

It is worth making an effort to learn something about how the tax system affects you and how investments are taxed. You don't have to become an expert, but just knowing how the system works makes it less likely that you will end up being over-taxed, or putting your money into an investment that isn't the best choice for you.

> Independent financial adviser and *Moneywise* Ask the Professionals panellist Rebekah Kearey says:
>
> "Avoiding tax is legal (as opposed to evading it, which isn't) and often increases income and the value of savings and investments. A basic knowledge of the tax rules will help you avoid unnecessary taxation and should prevent you inadvertently increasing your tax bill."

The biggest personal tax that affects most of us is income tax, which mainly comes from taxing our earnings. It makes up around a quarter of the government's total income. You may be surprised to learn that capital gains tax (CGT) and inheritance tax (IHT), which are often talked about, each make up less than 1% of the government's income. Part of the reason why CGT and IHT raise so little money is clever financial planning on the part of those people who might otherwise be liable to pay these taxes. We'll have a look at each of these taxes, how they might affect you, and explain how to minimise your bills or cut them out altogether.

When the Inland Revenue gets in touch, you need to check whether you've been given the right tax code if you pay tax through PAYE, and have filled in your tax return (if you're sent one) correctly. If you don't, you could end up paying too much tax.

This chapter will also deal with how your investments are taxed, so you'll have a clear idea of whether you've picked the most tax-efficient way to boost your income or save for the future. For historical reasons the tax year runs from 6 April one year to 5 April the next. The information in this book applies for the 1997/98 tax year.

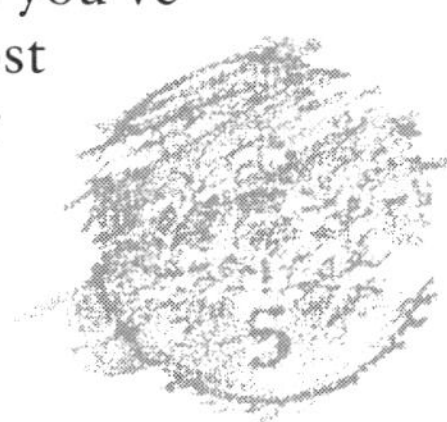

Income tax

THERE ARE THREE rates of income tax in 1997/98: 20%, 23% and 40%. Which investments you choose depend very much on which your top rate of tax is – for example, it's crucial for 40% taxpayers to pick tax-efficient investments.

TAX RATES FOR 1997/98

- *First £4,100 of taxable income:* tax paid at 20%
- *Next £4,100–£26,100 of taxable income:* 23%
- *More than £26,100 of taxable income:* 40%

The Chancellor has made it clear that he wants to see the lowest rate of tax dropping to 10p, so that may be good news for 1998 if your income is only just above the tax threshold.

Not all your income is taxable. We all (including children and retired people) have a personal tax allowance – an amount of income you can receive without paying any tax.

TAX-FREE ALLOWANCES

The first £4,045 of your income in 1997/98 is free of tax. Everyone who earns more money than that – for example, from investments or working, will probably have to pay tax on the extra money. On top of that allowance there are various other tax allowances which can reduce the total amount of tax you have to pay – the married couple's allowance, for example, currently gives married couples under 65 tax relief of 15% on £1,830, which means it's worth £274.50 (15% of the allowance) in tax savings to a couple in 1997/98. In effect that's a rather measly £137.25 each. There are also age-related allowances for older people, which can bring down tax bills in many cases.

The bulk of your income over £4,045 this year is potentially taxable – although there's a long list of investments and income that you don't have to pay any tax on (see opposite).

You claim all the allowances by filling in a tax return or writing to your tax office stating which allowances you're eligible for. See Dealing with the Inland Revenue on page 58.

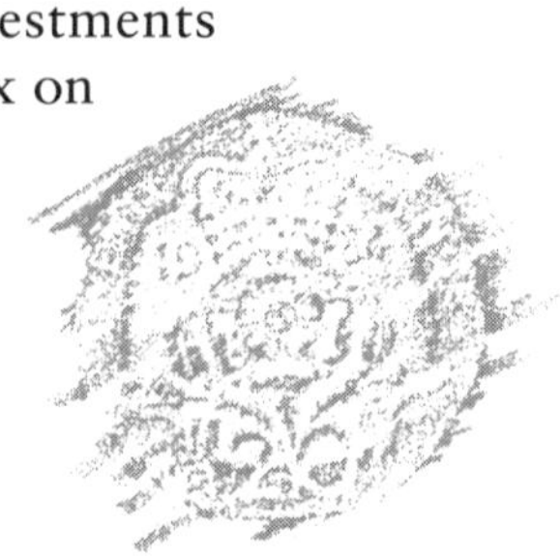

Main types of tax-free income

All the income and investments mentioned in this table don't carry any liability for income tax. It's especially important for 40% taxpayers (see below) to make sure that they have a range of tax-efficient investments from this list.

- Return from various National Savings investments: National Savings Certificates; Children's Bonus Bonds; Premium Bond prizes; the first £70 (or £140 if it's a joint account) interest a year from a National Savings ordinary account.
- Interest from a tax-exempt special savings account (TESSA).
- Return from a personal equity plan (PEP).
- Return from a tax-exempt Friendly Society plan.
- Part of the 'income' from a purchased annuity.
- Proceeds from Save As You Earn (SAYE) contracts.
- Profit-related pay under an approved scheme.
- A few fringe benefits you might get through your job.
- Up to £30,000 of redundancy pay.
- Maintenance payments you receive under court orders or other legally binding agreements made on or after 15 March 1988; the first part (£1,830 in 1997/98) of maintenance payments received under earlier court orders or binding agreements and any increases to such arrangements made after 5 April 1989; all voluntary maintenance payments.
- Income from life insurance paid out under a family income benefit policy.
- Some social security benefits.
- Betting winnings and lottery prizes.

TAX

MARRIED COUPLE'S ALLOWANCE

Couples who live together but aren't married can't claim the allowance. You have to be married and living at the same address as your spouse, but if one of you is away or working abroad you can still claim the allowance.

If you are getting married, you can claim the allowance for the rest of the tax year in which your wedding took place. The earlier in the tax year you get married, the more you can claim. If you get

Personal allowances for the 1997/98 tax year

Personal allowance		£4,045
Age allowance	for those aged 65–74	up to £5,220
	for those age 75 plus	up to £5,400

If you have an income of more than £15,600 you'll lose some of this allowance. Your extra allowance is reduced by £1 for every £2 of income that's over this amount. It can't go down below the normal £4,045 personal allowance. So, if you're between 65 and 74 you'll get only the usual allowances if your income is at least £17,950. If you're 75 or over, the break-even level is £18,310.

Married couple's allowance	for those aged under 65	£1,830
	Restricted to 15% relief, worth:	£274.50
	for those aged 65-74	£3,185
	Restricted to 15% relief, worth:	£477.75
	for those aged 75 plus	£3,225
	Restricted to 15% relief, worth:	£483.75
Additional personal allowance		£1,830
	Restricted to 15% relief, worth:	£274.50
Widow's bereavement allowance		£1,830
	Restricted to 15% relief, worth:	£274.50
Maintenance allowance		£1,830
	Restricted to 15% relief, worth:	£274.50

married between April 6th and May 5th you can claim the whole year's allowance.

When you get married one of you should contact your tax office. You'll find the address on your tax return. If you don't fill in a return, ask your employer to give you the telephone number and a company reference. You will be sent form 11PA, which allows you to choose to give all the allowance to one partner (the allowance will go to the man unless you specify otherwise) or split it equally. To split it, you need to tell the tax office that the wife is to get half or all the allowance – using form 18 (the tax office will send you one). You have to tell the Revenue before the start of the tax year for which you want

Example

If you get married on 8 June, you will have been married for ten months by the end of the tax year and so you'll be entitled to ten twelfths of the allowance. For the 1997/98 tax year the calculation is 10/12 X £1,830 = £1,525. Tax relief on this is £228·75.

the split to apply, and it will stay in place until you inform the Revenue you wish to change the arrangement by completing another form 18.

The higher married couple's allowance is payable whenever the older partner reaches 65. The catch is that the total amount of allowance you can deduct from your income has to be calculated on the husband's total income – even if it's his wife who is the older partner, and she's taking half the allowance.

Because married couples are now taxed separately you each have a higher personal allowance, so you can have an income of up to £15,600 (1997/98) each and claim the relevant higher tax allowance for your own age (see above). But any income over £15,600 reduces the higher allowance at a rate of £1 for every £2 of income, so if you have an income of £16,100, your allowance will be cut by £250. This makes it really important for pensioners to make the most of tax breaks and even out the income between them so that the husband, for example, uses up his higher age-related tax allowance, where the wife is a non-taxpayer.

You have to tell the Inland Revenue that your income is less than your personal allowance. For example, for a married man aged 65–74 this would be an income of less than £8,405 (higher personal allowance plus married couple's allowance) and for everyone else in that age group it would be an income of less than £5,220.

ADDITIONAL PERSONAL ALLOWANCE

If you are bringing up a child alone you can claim this allowance – marital status doesn't matter. A married man can claim if he's looking after children and his wife is incapacitated, but rather unfairly a wife can't claim if her husband is sick or disabled.

You must have at least one dependent child aged 16 or younger living with you. Children aged 16–18 who are still at school or college or are on a training course also count. If you're bringing up a child who isn't your natural child, you can still claim.

Where couples have split up, and both claim an allowance because the children spend time with both parents, then the tax relief is divided between them in agreed proportions, if they are still speaking. If you can't agree, the allowance is split according to how much time the children spend with each parent.

EXAMPLE

This shows how a typical tax bill is worked out. See Chapter 10 for more on tax relief on pensions and page 56 for details of tax and charity.

Income from your job	£36,000		
less charity donation via payroll giving	£1,200		
less contributions to pension scheme	£2,000		
		£32,800	
less personal allowance		£4,045	
taxable income	£29,035		
			tax
less £4,100 taxed at 20%		£4,100	£820
less £22,000 taxed at 23%		£22,000	£5,060
leaves £2,935 to be taxed at 40%		£2,935	£1,174
tax before married couple's allowance			£7,054·00
less married couple's allowance at 15% of £1,830			£274·50
TAX BILL			£6,779·50

WIDOW'S BEREAVEMENT ALLOWANCE

Women are eligible for this for the tax year in which their husbands die, and the following one (provided they don't remarry). The Revenue will also give a widow a full year's married couple's allowance for the year in which her husband died. There is no such allowance for widowers.

MAINTENANCE DEDUCTION

You are eligible for this if you're paying maintenance to an ex-spouse through a separation deed or a court order. If you make payments direct to your children, you can't get tax relief. You will get tax relief at 15% of the allowance through either a tax coding on your PAYE or a separate assessment, depending on your circumstances. Get a copy of leaflet IR93 if you think you might be entitled to this allowance.

Tax and your job

PAYE (Pay As You Earn) is the way most employees are paid. The tax is collected at the same time you are paid for your employment. You are issued with a PAYE code, which is an estimate of how much you can earn before you have to pay tax. You will be taxed on anything you earn on top of that, but your employer spreads your tax-free allowances throughout the year. The code appears on your payslip and is basically a shorthand way of stating what sort of taxpayer you are.

The Revenue arrives at the code by knocking off the last number of your tax-free allowance. So, the higher your code, the more tax-free income you will be allowed. If your tax circumstances change, for example, if you get married, or the Revenue think you've been paying too much or too little tax, then your tax code might change during the year. If that happens, you will be sent a coding notice explaining the changes and your employer will be told automatically, and adjust your tax accordingly.

It is quite likely you won't get a tax coding notice. Unless you are a higher-rate taxpayer or have got married recently, for example, you probably won't get one. The notice shows your code and on one side gives a list of the allowances and job expenses the Revenue thinks are due to you. It may also include pension contributions if you're a higher-rate taxpayer and items which qualify for tax relief, such as professional subscriptions.

The other side of the column shows what deductions have been made – for example, the restriction to the 15% fixed-relief allowances, taxable benefits through your work, such as private medical insurance, underpaid tax from previous years, and any taxable benefits you have had if you have been unemployed or off work.

The Revenue points out the important figures at the bottom of the note – the tax code it has given you for the year, and your tax-free allowances. If you are due for a tax refund, it will say so on the coding notice.

Perks

It's worth knowing how your perks will be taxed – they may seem less worthwhile once you realise that they aren't free! Some are tax-free, others only cost you money if you earn at a rate of more than £8,500 a year, while you have to pay tax on some perks regardless of your earnings.

What the tax coding letters mean

- **BR** All your earnings will be taxed at the basic rate because you've used up your allowances elsewhere (this code might be used if you have a second job).
- **D** All your earnings are taxed at the higher rate because you've used up your allowances elsewhere (again, probably used for a second job).
- **F** The tax due on another income, such as a pension, is being collected.
- **H** You get a personal allowance plus married couple's or another additional personal allowance.
- **K** If you have a K code, the amount shown on your tax code will be added to your tax bill rather than taken off it. You will get a K code if your taxable benefits and other income not taxed at source use up all your tax allowances.
- **L** You get the personal allowance.
- **NT** This appears if no tax is due from your pay packet.
- **P** If you are a single pensioner aged 65-74.
- **T** This is used in most other cases. For example, if you are 75 or more and get a personal allowance; if you are 65 or more but get a reduced age allowance because your income is above a certain level; if you have a company car; if you don't want your employer to know your marital status or age.
- **V** If you are a married pensioner likely to be paying basic-rate tax.

- *Free perks*: These include free life insurance, drinks and meals provided free by your employer, pension contributions from your employer and season ticket loans of less than £5,000 a year.
- *Those earning at a rate of more than £8,500*: These people must pay tax on perks including the taxable value of a car, child-care vouchers and medical insurance. There are lots of rules covering company cars – talk it through with your employer if you're not sure how much you are being taxed. If you are given a choice between cash or a car, remember you have to pay tax on the cash as well as on the taxable value of the car.

Your payslip

A payslip shows how your gross pay has shrunk into your take-home (net) pay. It shows your tax payment for the month and usually for the tax year to date. It also shows how much National Insurance is being paid by you and your employer.

- *EE NI*: Employee's National Insurance contributions.
- *ER NI*: Your employer's payments.

There are also boxes for other deductions from your pay, such as pension contributions or payroll giving. These should be spelled out in full, so you can see how much is being taken away.

If you work for yourself, you won't pay tax through PAYE – you have to complete a tax return every year. You need to keep full and accurate records of your business transactions. You pay tax on your annual profits. You can choose the 12-month period you want to be your 'accounting year'.

Previously if you were self-employed you paid tax for a specific tax year on the profits for your accounting year ending the previous tax year. For the 1996/97 tax year, there are transitional rules. You pay tax on the average profit for the two years ending in the 1996/97 tax year. For 1997/98 you pay tax on your profit to 30 June 1997.

You have to make two payments on account towards your tax bill each year: one on 31 January and one on 31 July. If there is more tax to pay, you need to pay it on the following 31 January. For 1997/98 the payments are based on your tax bill for the previous tax year 1996/97. If it turns out that you should have paid more than this, you'll pay the extra on 31 January 1999 – if you shouldn't have paid as much, you should get your repayment on that date.

Your profits for tax purposes will probably be slightly different to your 'real' profits, as not all expenses are deductible under tax rules, for example. If you make a loss you may be able to use it to reduce your tax bill by setting it against other income or future profits.

Another tax you may have to deal with when you work for yourself is VAT – value added tax. If your business is a certain size you have to register with Customs & Excise. You may decide to register, even if it's not compulsory, as it could mean saving money.

SAVINGS AND INVESTMENTS

Many investments have already been taxed at the lower rate of 20%, before you receive the interest or proceeds. If you are a 20% or 23% taxpayer, there is nothing more to pay. If you are a higher-rate taxpayer you have to pay tax at 40% on all taxable income, so if you are an employee you may find that your tax code is changed to take account of the extra money you owe to the Revenue. (As soon as you become a higher-rate taxpayer, you will get a tax return, and you will have to mention all your taxable investments on that, so that you're charged the right amount of extra tax.) With savings accounts, the interest is paid net of tax at 20% but if you are a non-taxpayer you can choose to have it paid gross. You will need to fill in a form (form R85), which you can get from a bank or building society.

Charity

There are various tax-efficient ways to give to charity. These benefit both you and your chosen charities. A deed of covenant is a legally binding agreement to give part of your income to a charity each year. It attracts tax relief if you sign up for over three years. Give As You Earn (GAYE) schemes allow employees to get income tax relief at their top rate on donations of up to £900 a year. The money is paid to the charity from your gross pay. Under Gift Aid you can get tax relief on gifts to charity of at least £250. You claim the relief through your tax return. So you have to pay a net amount of at least £250.

Capital gains tax and Inheritance tax

- Capital gains tax (CGT) is charged when you make a big profit from the sale of an investment or asset (don't worry, your house is the one major exception to this rule). You have a CGT allowance every year (£6,500 in 1997/98) and you can make that much profit on sales of assets before any tax is payable.
- Inheritance tax (IHT) is a death tax, paid out of the dead person's estate or by his or her heirs. You can leave up to £215,000 in your estate before any tax has to be paid.

How to avoid CGT

There's plenty of scope for avoiding a CGT bill as there are many exemptions to the CGT rules.

The points below cover the main rules at the moment, but the Chancellor has made it clear that he is going to crack down on tax avoidance in future, so some of these tax breaks may be lost. Keep an eye on the Budget statements to check on any changes to CGT rules.

- Some assets, notably your house, are exempt from CGT.
- You can ignore any gain you've made that's due to inflation.
- You have an annual allowance that allows you to make a profit (£6,500 this year) before you're liable for tax.
- *If you transfer some of your assets to your spouse,* they are exempt from this tax.
- Even if you have made what's called a chargeable gain on your investments, there are several sorts of reliefs available which can help you avoid a bill. They include:
- Reinvestment relief, where you sell one asset and reinvest in unquoted shares of small companies. It's risky, but it defers your tax bill until you eventually sell the shares.
- Retirement relief, which is payable to people who retire and sell some business assets.

How to avoid IHT

Again, this is a tax which is not likely to be a problem for most people. It is paid on some gifts you give away during the final years of your life and what you have left after your death. If your estate is worth less than £215,000, there is no tax to pay.

The points below cover the main IHT rules at the moment, but expect changes. This is one area where the government would find it easy to claw back more tax, by changing the rules on giving away gifts during the final years of your life, for example. At the moment you can give away your money and assets, and if you live for seven years afterwards your heirs (or the estate) don't have to pay any tax on them. This would be an easy rule to abolish.

Essentially, IHT planning is something you are doing for the benefit of your heirs. You won't see any benefit from it in your lifetime, so be careful not to give so much of your money and possessions away that you end up in a vulnerable position. Trusts can play an important part in tax planning if you're wealthy or have a complicated family life. For a more detailed assessment

> Independent financial adviser and *Moneywise* Ask the Professionals panellist Rebekah Kearey says:
>
> "It is never too early to start inheritance tax planning. The current threshold may seem high now, but future legislation may alter the situation. It is surprising how quickly assets start to build in value once you include things like property.
>
> Early planning often allows you to use the cheapest options and maintain greater flexibility."

of IHT and tax planning, turn to Chapter 11.

In brief, there's no inheritance tax to pay on the following:

- Gifts made between a husband and wife are always exempt from tax, so you can leave everything to your spouse.
- Gifts to any number of people, so long as they don't get more than £250 each.
- You can give away up to £3,000 a year in other gifts to family and friends.
- Cash gift of £5,000 to a child who is getting married.
- Any other gift you give won't be liable for tax if you live for seven years after transferring ownership.
- Gifts to charities and other public bodies, as well as political parties and housing associations.

YOUR FINANCES

Dealing with the Inland Revenue

In the past you might have had to deal with several different Inland Revenue offices for different aspects of your finances. Now your tax affairs should be handled by one tax office. If the Revenue hasn't been able to organise this in your case, it will provide you with one point of contact, so that any chasing around is done by the Revenue, not you.

- If you're employed, your employer will be able to tell you the name and address of your tax office – if you move jobs, your tax office may change.
- If you become unemployed you stay with the tax office relating to your last employer.
- If you're self-employed or in a partnership, your tax office is usually the one nearest to where you work. If your income is from an employers pension, your tax office will probably be the one in the area where the pension fund office is. If it's only a small pension or your only pension is from the State, it will be the office in the area where you live.
- If your only income is from a personal pension, your tax office will be the one which covers the pension provider.
- If your only income is from investments, then the office will depend on where you live.

Tax returns

Not everyone gets a tax return. About nine million people were sent them in 1997, and that number is mostly made up of self-employed people, people who work in partnerships, higher-rate taxpayers, and some pensioners. So don't worry if you haven't seen a tax return – people who are employed basic-rate taxpayers won't necessarily get one.

If you are employed but get a separate income from, say, investments or from a second job, then you should ask the Revenue for a tax return – even if you haven't been sent one. The onus is on you to tell the Revenue about any income or capital gains that they don't know about, within six months of the end of the relevant tax year. If you don't do this, you might get landed with a big tax bill.

> **Tip**
> Keep every piece of paper relevant to your income or any capital gains from sales that you've made. If you don't keep your records straight and do not have evidence to back up your tax claim then you could end up being fined up to £3,000 for each failure.

There is a new tax return system which allows you to calculate your own tax liability if you want to – and that's why it's called self assessment. But there's no reason for you to have to work it out yourself because the Revenue will still do all the sums for you. If you want them to do the assessment, you have to fill in your forms and send them back before the end of September each year. In this way, employed people who owe less than £1,000 in tax can also ask for it to be paid via PAYE rather than in a lump sum.

If you are happy to calculate your own tax liability, you can delay returning your tax return until the end of January – but you must send a cheque at the same time. If you miss this deadline you'll be fined £100 automatically, plus another £100 if you hang on to the return for a further six months.

Your new basic tax return is 8 pages long. The forms for the current 1997/98 tax year, which have to be returned by the end of January 1998 (see above) cover the tax year to April 5 1997 and allow you to claim allowances for the current tax year, ending April 1998. As well as the basic forms, you'll get supplementary pages relevant to your personal tax position. There are several sets of pages:

- Income from employment.
- Partnerships.
- Share schemes.

- Self-employment.
- Owning land and buildings.
- Foreign income.
- Income from trusts.
- Income from capital gains.
- Forms for non-UK residents.

The tax assessment system is new and will be refined in years to come. But the basic steps are as follows:

1. Check you have all the right pages from the Revenue. Go through the documents and see if there is anything else you may want to send for – including help sheets and tax leaflets. The Revenue's order line will take your calls on 0645 000404. You can order a computerised version of the forms on the same number.
2. Collect all your supporting documents. This might include a P11D if you are in employment and receiving taxable benefits, and a P60 form showing your pay for the year and tax paid under PAYE. If you've worked for more than one employer during the year, you should have a P60 for each employment and you should also get one showing any benefits payments such as Jobseeker's Allowance.
3. Fill in the forms or pay someone else to do it for you. If you already use an accountant he or she will help with the tax return. Many people are being bombarded with offers from services offering to fill in tax returns, most of which cost around £100, including VAT. The catch is that a lot of them will only accept customers who have uncomplicated tax affairs. Once you've read through the forms, and the accompanying guide, you should be able to fill them in yourself. Call the Inland Revenue Helpline on 0645 000444 for more help – the operators can tell you where to put relevant figures but they won't help you fill in the return.

Problems

If you disagree with something on your payslip, contact your employer. Anything else, such as a wrong tax code or a mistake on a tax bill, has to go via the Revenue.

- If you want some general help or advice, without speaking to your own tax inspector initially, contact one of the network of Tax Enquiry Centres. You can make an appointment if you want to discuss something in detail. The name and address of your nearest centre will be in the phone book under Inland Revenue. You'll also find the number for your local Revenue office – it may not be responsible for your tax, but the officials there may be able to help you. You can also pick up a range of tax books and leaflets at enquiry centres and local offices.

> **TIP**
> Tax inspectors are human, and do make mistakes. Keep copies of everything you send to the Revenue, and make sure they know your current address – even if you've told your employer that you've moved this won't be passed on to your tax office.

- If you disagree with the tax assessment the Revenue has calculated for you, then you should contact your tax office within 30 days and ask to postpone payment of the tax in dispute. The tax inspector named on your assessment form should deal with the case. If you can't agree on the amount, then the case may have to go on to the tax commissioners. There are general and specialist tax commissioners around, who deal with tax problems of varying complexity. The general commissioners, who are knowledgeable lay people advised by an expert clerk, tend to deal with most personal tax disputes.

  The specialist commissioners deal with the most complex cases. Unless your problem hinges on a point of law, the commissioners' decision is final and you won't be able to take it forward if you disagree with their ruling. A case where a point of law is disputed will go to the Court of Appeal.
- If you feel you have been let down by administrative errors at the tax office, you can complain direct. If you and your tax inspector can't agree, take the problem to the district inspector of taxes. There will also be a regional inspector if you are still upset after exhausting other channels.

Action plan

- Make sure that you are receiving all the allowances to which you might be entitled.
- If you have not checked your tax code, do so. If you believe that it is incorrect, contact your tax office and tell them why you think this. Check the tax you have paid in previous years as well.

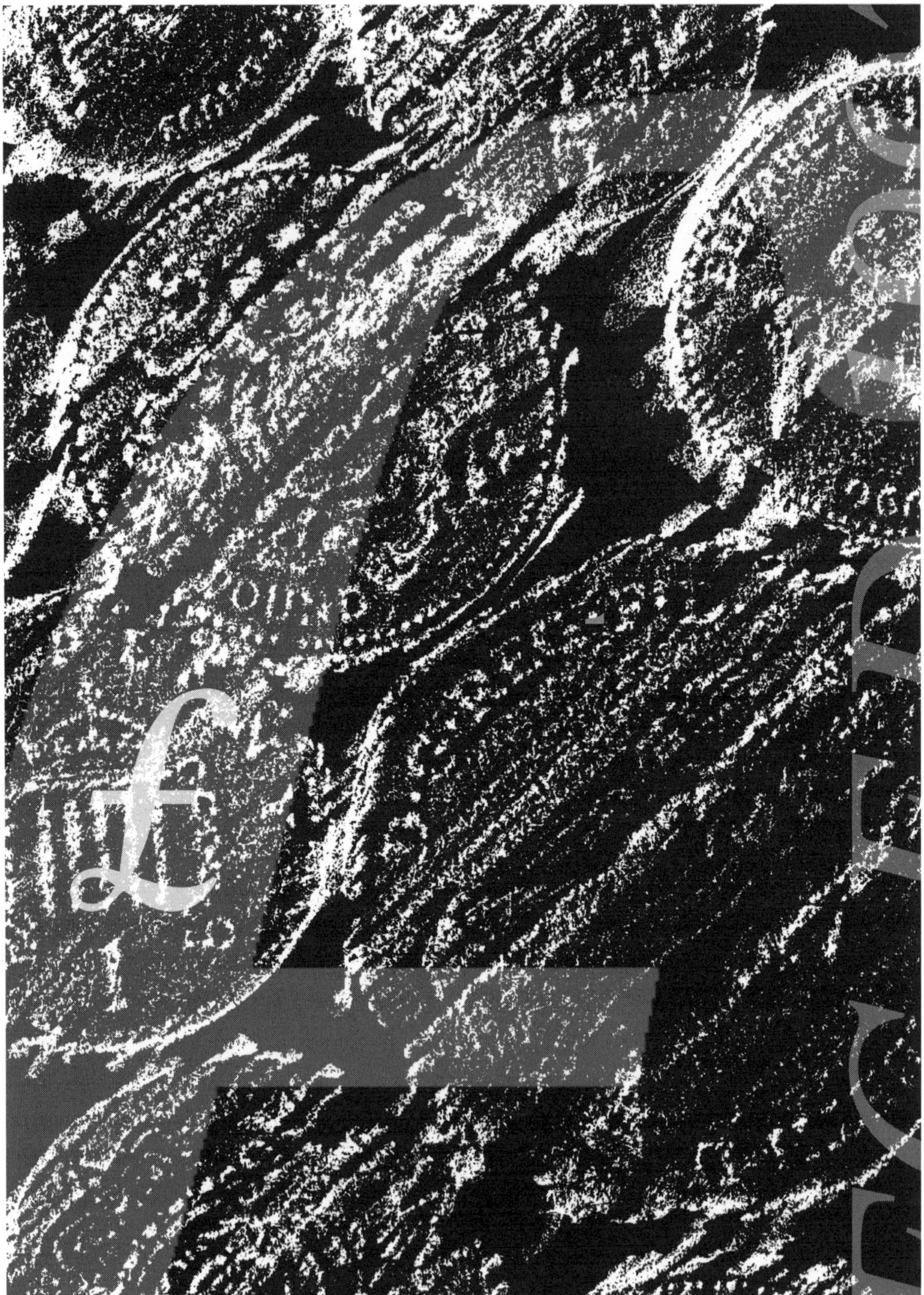

5 Mortgages

When you buy a home you want to get everything right – you want to choose the right property, the right solicitor, the right removal company … and the right mortgage. The right property and the right mortgage are obviously the most important as you're going to have to live with your choice. You can switch your mortgage before the term is up, but there are costs involved so it's better to get it right first time and only change if circumstances mean a different option would make you better off.

Paying for housing is a massive expense so you need to make sure you get a good deal to leave some cash available for the other financial planning needs covered in the following chapters.

In this chapter we'll look at the reasons why you might want to step on the housing ladder for the first time, exactly how to buy a house, which mortgage to pick, and, for experienced homeowners, how to switch your mortgage if you aren't getting the best deal. There's also a case for paying off part or all of the capital you owe on your mortgage, and we'll tell you when and how to do it.

The first time

IT'S ALMOST AUTOMATICALLY ASSUMED that we'll buy a home as an 'investment' in our late twenties or early thirties, and carry the debt for the rest of our working lives. But is a mortgage a good investment? Millions of people who bought homes in the inflated market of the late 1980s found themselves stuck with a home worth less than the mortgage when prices slumped a few years later. As this book was published the market was booming again, with prices rising fastest in London and the South East.

If you are thinking about buying for the first time, you need to ask yourself some important questions. Don't listen to those who tell you that renting a home is 'throwing money down the drain'. Everyone's case is different and you have to work out whether buying a house would offer you more benefits than your current rental arrangement. Go through this checklist and work out whether you still want to buy.

Do you have a very low rent?
If you do, it might make more sense to save as much as you can and wait a while before buying a home. More savings mean a bigger deposit and a better deal when you eventually buy a house.

Can you see yourself staying in the house for at least six years?
If not, don't buy. Lots of people had their fingers burnt in the 1980s when they bought tiny studio flats as the first step on the property ladder. Now those flats are hard to sell because lots of people wait longer before they buy their first home – until they're 31 on average. They've got more money, so studios and one-bedroomed flats are being by-passed as first-timers go for larger homes.

Are you buying with someone else?
You'll get more for your money because you can share the costs. Lenders will give two people a loan that adds up to 2·5 times their joint salary, which generally adds up to more than the three times salary loan they'll give to a single person. In addition, there are two of you to pay for lawyers, arrangement fees and all the other costs when you first get a mortgage.

That's the upside. Don't even think about buying as a couple if you're in a relationship that's shaky. And don't buy with a friend without a clear agreement about when, or under what circumstances, you'd sell up. We get lots of letters at *Moneywise* from people who've taken out joint mortgages and then found themselves alone and left to pay the whole cost. They can't understand why they can't just pay their own 'half' of the monthly payments. Unfortunately, there's little we can do to help except to suggest a speedy sale of the house or taking in a lodger. You're jointly liable for a mortgage you take out with someone else, so if he or she leaves and refuses to make any more repayments, you have the choice of getting behind on repayments – and risk having the house repossessed – or finding the whole lot yourself.

Are you going to buy a home in an area where property prices are likely to go up?
This calls for judgement on your part. If you're serious about buying you will already be familiar with what you can get in your area for the amount you can afford. Prices may be on a roll, but you need to ask yourself whether the area is considered 'desirable'? The old estate agent's mantra of 'location, location and location' is really important. If you are pretty sure you could sell a home in your chosen area at a profit when you need to move on, then you should really consider buying.

Step-by-step guide to buying your home

STEP ONE: DECIDE HOW MUCH YOU CAN AFFORD TO SPEND

Before you start house-hunting, visit the bank or building society and find out how much you can afford to spend on a house. You can do a rough estimate by multiplying your salary by three, adding on any deposit you've saved. If you are buying with a partner you should add your salaries together and multiply the total by 2·5.

That's straightforward enough. The problem comes when one or both of you has an unpredictable work pattern: perhaps you're on a short-term contract, or have changed jobs several times in the last few years.

If one of you is self-employed, most lenders will want to see three years of accounts. Be prepared for a battle: as a self-employed person you'll be trying to set as much of your income against tax as you can to reduce your total tax bill. That makes your income look low, so you'll need to work hard to get a loan for more than that.

Lenders hate unconventional people and most of them have yet to wake up to the fact that working patterns have changed. If you know you don't fit into a neat pigeonhole and your existing bank or building society won't offer you a deal, you may do well to avoid the high street and use a firm of mortgage brokers, which will have access to every mortgage on the market.

There is a snag – you'll have to pay for their services and this can cost several hundred pounds. (You can reduce or cut this out if you take out insurance or buy an endowment mortgage as the broker will earn commission.) Don't be afraid to pay: a good deal from a broker can save you hundreds of pounds a year in mortgage costs. Ask around for recommendations – at the moment brokers aren't regulated and some firms offer a much better service than others.

You get tax relief on mortgage interest payments, which may affect the amount you decide to spend. The value of tax relief has been cut gradually over recent years and looks set to be cut further. In effect, you get a discount of 15% on the interest that you pay on the first £30,000 of your mortgage. The discount goes down to 10% from April 1998.

> **Tip**
> In an over-heated housing market you should get yourself approved for a mortgage deal before you make an offer on a property. This will maximise the advantage you already have as a first-time buyer, and you'll be able to make a speedy deal on your dream home.

Step Two: Budget for all the extra costs involved in buying a house

These will depend entirely on how much you intend to borrow. Add up the likely costs from the list below. Stick to a pessimistic estimate – any money left over will be eaten up as soon as you move in as there's always something that needs doing.

A survey of the property you want to buy costs a lot of money and, as there's no guarantee you'll buy the property, it could be money down the drain. Once you've had an offer accepted you have to have the property surveyed and the lender has to agree to lend on the basis of what the survey says.

You may have to pay out more money if the lender refuses to give you a loan until, for example, you have a damp course put in. If the survey shows up something radically wrong with the place, you may be able to knock down the purchase price to take account of what you'll have to spend on repairs. But when it's a seller's market, the vendor may refuse to reduce the price.

There are three types of survey. Spend as much as you can, although realistically a homebuyer's report will provide you with all the essential information, and it gives you the basis for a claim against a surveyor who fails to spot a major defect. The lender will appoint a surveyor to carry out the type of report you want:

Valuation report: This is prepared for the lender, although you have to pay for it. The surveyor only gives the property a visual inspection. You can't claim against a surveyor who misses something important unless it's absolutely obvious and serious: a ceiling has collapsed, for example. Cost: about £50.

Homebuyer's report: This is prepared for you, although the lender sees a copy. It's more detailed than a valuation report, and this is the minimum type of survey you should have prepared. Cost: about £250. Check.

Full structural survey: This is the full works and it will probably scare you! It will go into some detail, and, if you can afford it, it's worth having done. A full survey is a must if you are buying a period property. Cost: £500 plus.

Conveyancing: is the process of transferring a home from one owner to another. A solicitor or a licensed conveyancer will carry out a detailed search through the local authority and Land Registry records. This will turn up any nasty surprises that might put you off buying the house – for example, the lovely field behind your dream cottage might be earmarked as a site for a new bypass. Costs: about £300–£400 including VAT for the conveyancing, plus local searches – up to £125, plus Land Registry searches and fees. These depend on the property price and can be anything from £50–£250.

Stamp duty: This tax has to be paid when you buy a house costing £60,000 or more. In the July 1997 Budget two new levels were introduced. Stamp duty will be charged at 1·5% of the sale price if it is over £250,000 and at 2% if it costs £500,000 or more. If the sale price is between £60,000 and £250,000 you pay 1% of the total sale price. If you buy a leasehold flat the stamp duty you pay depends on the ground rent. Cost: between 1% and 2% of the total price of the flat or house.

Buying kitchen appliances, curtains and carpets from the existing homeowners: Read the house details carefully when you look round a property. Anything that is not a fixed part of the home but is mentioned in the details must be included in the purchase price. So, for example, if the kitchen details mention a fridge, that is included, but the details may also say the kitchen is 'plumbed for a washing machine'. That means you'll have to buy your own or make an offer for the existing washing machine. The vendors will let your lawyer know which items they are willing to sell, and at what price. Be prepared to haggle. The owners may well want to get rid of most of the stuff anyway, especially curtains and carpets. Cost: anything from nothing up to £1,000.

Arrangement fees and insurance policies: These are the hidden 'stings' in lots of mortgages. You may have to pay simply to arrange a fixed-rate or discounted mortgage, for example, and then you may be asked to take out buildings and/or contents insurance as a condition of getting the loan. Even if you don't have to buy insurance from your lender, you'll need to arrange your own policies as buildings insurance is usually a pre-condition of the loan. You have to insure the house at its 'reinstatement value', which is how much it would cost to rebuild completely. Then there's life insurance – you may want to get a term insurance policy, which will pay off whatever is left of your loan if you die during the term of the mortgage. Some lenders demand that you have life insurance for a repayment mortgage, others don't. Cost: arrangement fee – £100–£750. Buildings and contents insurance – depends on the value of the house and contents; budget from £20 a month upwards. Term assurance – depends on your age; from £10 a month upwards.

Mortgage indemnity guarantee (MIG): This is a payment you may have to make to protect the lender against loss if you default on the mortgage. Most lenders charge MIG on a rising scale on any figure you borrow above 75% of the purchase price. It is a one-off payment that you can either pay upfront or add to the mortgage loan. But a MIG payment doesn't mean that you are covered if you fail to keep up mortgage repayments and hand the property back to the lender. The lender can still pursue you for all the debt still owing. Cost: up to £1,000 or more.

Step Three: Decide what sort of mortgage you want

A mortgage is a loan that allows you to buy a house or flat and then pay the money back, plus interest, over many years. The best way to approach your decision is to decide whether you want to pay back the capital and interest on your loan as part of a single package, or whether you prefer to make monthly interest payments and take out a second investment plan to pay off the capital at the end of the mortgage term.

First-time buyers will be offered special deals, but these may not suit your circumstances. If you're buying for the second time or remortgaging, it is also worth looking at flexible mortgages (see page 74 for our advice on re-mortgaging).

Once you've made that decision you have to work out what interest-rate arrangement you want to fix up with the lender. The basic choices are capped, fixed or discounted loans, which give you peace of mind by protecting the amount you have to pay every month (for a few years), or taking out a mortgage that has to be repaid at the bank's standard lending rate. That rate will move up and down with interest rates.

Repayment method

Mortgages seem confusing and some lenders don't really help much: information leaflets are confusing and use ridiculous jargon. Make sure you get on well with your mortgage adviser and don't be afraid to ask questions. The bottom line is that there are only two ways to pay for a mortgage loan, so you need to decide which suits you best.

Repayment mortgage

A straightforward loan, set up so that you pay off part of both the capital and interest owed every month.

Advantages: Monthly payments are calculated to make sure that you pay off everything you owe at the end of the mortgage term. If you worry about risk, this sort of mortgage gives you peace of mind. If you get into difficulty, you can usually reduce your monthly costs by extending the number of repayment years.

> **Tip**
> When you take out a repayment loan, make sure the mortgage is transferable to a new property.

Disadvantages: You need to be very careful if you move house within a few years of taking out the mortgage. In the early years most of your repayments are interest only and you won't have paid back any of the capital you owe. If you then move and take out a new mortgage you might end up having made no progress towards paying off the loan.

Some people like an element of investment built into their mortgage. You don't get that with a repayment mortgage, it's just a loan.

There is no life cover, so you'll probably have to buy that separately.

Interest-only mortgages

All other forms of repaying your loan will mean you have to make monthly payments that only cover the interest on the loan. This sort of mortgage should be backed up with some form of investment designed to pay off the capital owing at the end of the 25-year term – or perhaps sooner. In the current housing boom there have been reports of people who have taken out an interest-only mortgage but are relying on the rise in house prices so that they can sell at a profit and pay off the capital when they move on. This is a very risky approach! There are several investments accepted as ways to repay your capital:

Endowment policies

A with-profits endowment is still the most popular way to pay off your mortgage. It is an investment policy with an element of life insurance. Your money goes into the life company's funds and is invested in a combination of cash, gilts, bonds, property, equities, and so on. But the varying performance of these investments is smoothed out for you because the policy only grows once a year. This annual bonus is often called a reversionary bonus. When your policy matures you will get a terminal bonus as well. The idea is that you'll get enough to pay off your mortgage, plus an extra lump sum.

Advantages: If you keep the endowment going for 25 years there is an excellent chance it will pay off the capital and leave you with some extra cash.

If you get a lump sum you can pay off the capital on your mortgage and keep the endowment running as a straight investment policy.

Once the policy has been running for several years it is valuable to other investors. If you no longer need the endowment,

> Independent mortgage adviser and *Moneywise* Ask the Professionals panellist Walter Avrili says:
>
> "Endowment policies can offer good value if critical illness insurance is added to the death benefit. The ability to contribute to the endowment no matter how many times you move or remortgage can be attractive."

Independent mortgage adviser and *Moneywise* Ask the Professionals panellist Walter Avrili says:

"It is always better to keep an endowment until maturity. If you are forced to stop paying, you have a number of options provided your mortgage lender agrees. You can just stop paying the premiums but leave the money invested until the maturity date; you could surrender the policy – but this probably won't give you good value; or you can sell or auction the policy."

or have to sell it for financial or personal reasons, you can sell it on to a dealer for a good price.

Endowments have life insurance built in so your mortgage will be paid off if you die.

Disadvantages: Endowments generate lots of commission for the person who sells you the policy, whereas a repayment mortgage offers salespeople measly payment. That's why endowments are so popular! Be cynical about the reasons why they are offering you an endowment.

There's really no point in taking out an endowment if you are not sure about your future plans. Remember, you have to keep paying into the policy for 25 years. If you cash it in during the early years you'll probably get back less than you put in. Couples who divorce are especially vulnerable to losing out on endowments.

In addition, there's no guarantee that the endowment will pay off the capital. If it doesn't, you will have to make up the shortfall.

Unit-linked endowments

A unit-linked endowment is invested in a specific stockmarket fund or funds. These policies go up and down in line with fund performance.

Advantages: None that you wouldn't be able to get more cheaply from a PEP (see below).

Disadvantages: You can't sell an unwanted unit-linked endowment to a dealer.

If share prices are low when your policy matures you won't get a very good return for all your years of investment.

TIP
Don't bother with a unit-linked endowment policy. Depending on your attitude to risk, a with-profits endowment or a PEP would be more suitable.

PEPs

This sort of repayment scheme takes advantage of the tax breaks available to private investors who buy shares. You pay into an approved personal equity plan (PEP) every month and, over the long term, your investment should show excellent returns. You get all the proceeds free of any tax. But it is not for the faint-hearted or those who want a mortgage they can forget about: you need to keep an eye on how your investments are growing, to make sure they are on course to pay off the mortgage capital. If necessary you can switch between PEP providers.

Advantages: Excellent potential if you pick a good PEP fund. You may be able to pay off the mortgage capital early.

If you have to sell up during a slump in the market you can cash in your PEP and pay off any negative equity – the gap between the sale value of your home and the capital you still owe.

You can extend the term of the mortgage if you are having trouble meeting payments.

Disadvantages: The investment returns can vary from year to year. If you want to see a steady rise, you should get a with-profits endowment.

You can't take out another PEP for general investment purposes during that year but the future of PEPs is uncertain after 1999, so it's not for the cautious.

There's no life cover, so you may have to buy that separately.

Pensions

Not a popular option, but a tax-efficient one. You pay into a pension plan and use the lump sum from the pension scheme when you retire to pay off the capital you owe. Personal pensions and some company pensions are accepted by lenders.

Advantages: Lots of tax advantages. You get tax relief on the pension contributions and they grow tax-free like a normal pension. Any life insurance you take out through the pension qualifies for the same tax relief.

Disadvantages: This option ties up your pension lump sum, although you could always pay off the capital using other savings if the opportunity arose.

If you have an unpredictable income and work pattern this isn't for you.

A PEP is more flexible as you can pay off the capital early – you don't have to wait for a lump sum at retirement.

Interest payment

WHEN YOU'VE DECIDED how you want to repay the loan, you have to decide what sort of interest-rate package you want from a lender.

TIP
When you start shopping around for a discount deal, be on the lookout for a realistic discount together with a short lock-in period when the discount comes to an end.

DISCOUNTS
Typically, these offer a percentage off the variable rate for a number of years. You see some amazing discounted rates in the newspapers, but pay careful attention to the small print. After the deal ends you'll be locked into paying a standard variable rate mortgage for anything from a few months up to two years.

FIXED RATES
These are fashionable when interest rates seem to be on a general upward trend. The attraction of a fixed rate is that it leaves you free to plan your finances up to six years ahead, knowing exactly what your repayments will be. The snag is that you may be caught on the hop if interest rates come down, and you're paying over the odds. In addition, lenders want to lock you in for the maximum length of time if they have sold you a low-interest deal, and they won't allow you any extra repayments against the capital outstanding on your loan.

CAPPED MORTGAGES
Your mortgage rate rises and falls in line with interest rates under a 'ceiling' agreed at the outset. Even if interest rates shoot up, your repayments can only go up to a fixed maximum. This sort of deal protects you against a big hike in rates. It also means that if interest rates fall below your capped rate, you end up paying less.

DEFERRED REPAYMENT LOANS
Last seen in the 1980s, these mortgages are making a comeback at the edges of acceptable lending practices. They are designed to entice young buyers who don't have much money by allowing them to defer any repayments for a year or so. But this extra money is added to the loan, with interest. Avoid.

STANDARD VARIABLE RATE MORTGAGES

Your mortgage payments will rise and fall along with interest rates, exposing you to extremes. However, if you want to pay off some of the capital owing on your mortgage – known as partial redemption – you will only be able to do it with a variable rate deal. You may be best off with a flexible mortgage (see page 77). There's no need to suffer a high variable rate if you have no intention of paying off some of the mortgage capital. Look around for a remortgage and work out whether the savings outweigh the costs.

A better mortgage deal?

IF YOU'RE AN existing borrower you might be able to get a better deal elsewhere; you don't have to stick with one lender for 25 years.

Ask yourself the following questions and if you answer 'Yes' to all of them you should look around and try saving money by renegotiating your loan.

- ❍ Does your mortgage represent 75% or less of your property's value?
- ❍ Is your mortgage for £30,000 or more?
- ❍ Are you paying the lender the standard variable rate or more?

When you remortgage you're simply taking your debt and moving it from one lender to another. Decide whether you want to go for a fixed rate or any other special deal (see page 73). There are also discounted variable rate deals available from lenders who run their operations by phone. The cost of swapping your loan to one of these lenders should be less than taking up a branch-based deal.

> Independent mortgage adviser and *Moneywise* Ask the Professionals panellist Walter Avrili says:
>
> "Many of the quality remortgage deals offer assistance with the cost of remortgaging, which could be up to £800. You need to understand the full conditions of a mortgage – compulsory redemption penalties, insurance and fees. You can only tell if a switch is worthwhile by doing this."

Whatever your plans, approach your existing lender first and ask if it will offer you a new deal. If you get no joy at first, it's worth going back after you've checked what offers you can get from other lenders. The mortgage market is very competitive and once your bank or building society sees that you're serious about changing to a new lender, you may get a better response. Bear in mind that there are quite a few costs involved in switching. When you've found a deal that looks attractive, work through the remortgaging calculator on page 76 to make sure a switch is worthwhile.

Paying off some or all of your mortgage

IT'S TEMPTING TO IMAGINE a life without mortgage payments. If you inherit a lump sum, for example, you might consider paying off some or all the capital you owe to buy your home outright.

Answer the following questions before you make your decision:

Do you want to lock the cash away in your home?

If you're not sure, there are ways round this – such as a flexible mortgage, which allows you to take the money out again if you need it. See page 77 for more details.

How much return are you getting on the money where it's invested at the moment?

There's usually a gap of at least 2% between the highest gross savings rates you will get at building society and the standard mortgage rate. It's not surprising, as banks and building societies make their money by lending you money at a higher interest rate than they are paying the savers. This means someone with all their savings in the building society may do well to pay off some capital, especially if he or she is a higher-rate taxpayer. However, if you've got tax-free investments that are performing well, the total return may be more than the current interest rate you're paying on the mortgage.

You have to decide whether you're happier to leave that investment alone, which may carry the risk that the stockmarket will fall, rather than remove the risk by using the money to pay off a home loan now.

Remortgaging calculator

Before you switch your mortgage you need to make sure it is worthwhile changing. Use the calculator below to work out how much it will cost you

	First year	Rest of offer period	Longer term
ADD UP WHAT YOU WILL SAVE:			
Cashback			
Yearly savings on			
Monthly repayments			
Other savings (e.g. free insurance)			
TOTAL			
DEDUCT WHAT YOU WILL SPEND:			
Paid to existing lender: Early redemption penalty			
Administration costs (e.g. deeds fee, sealing fee)			
Mortgage discharge fee			
Interest between last payment and end of month			
Paid to new lender: Arrangement fee			
Valuation fee			
Mortgage protection fee			
More expensive insurance			
Other extra insurance			
Legal fees: Your own solicitor			
New lender's solicitor			
Search fees			
Land registry fees			
Other charges			
Total			
Surplus/deficit			

Flexible mortgages

THIS IS A RELATIVELY new way to repay your loan and it's worth knowing about. These mortgages are designed to save you money by cutting the number of years left before you pay off the loan. You can save thousands of pounds with little effort, and you'll be free to concentrate on other investments and retirement planning.

You can treat your flexible mortgage account like a savings account. Most of these loans allow you to put in lump sums, or overpay every month to cut your mortgage term from 25 to 20 or even 15 years. If you need the money again, you can take it out. Some lenders will let you have a cheque book and cashcard, so you can treat the mortgage account like any other bank account. These loans are especially good for people who have unpredictable incomes, are expecting a lump sum, or who are aiming to pay extra loan repayments every month. If you have a 'store' of extra money built up you can miss repayments – for example, because one partner is taking a career break to have children.

Most lenders offering these loans want people in their thirties, forties and fifties who have paid off at least 30% of what they owe. Big players in this market include Bank of Scotland, Legal & General and Yorkshire Bank. It is advisable to compare what several lenders have to offer before you commit to a remortgage. You can take out a flexible deal on a repayment basis only or for an interest only loan.

Action plan

- ❍ If you are a first-time buyer, run through our checklist on page 64 to make sure you're really ready to buy.
- ❍ Whether you're a first-time buyer or moving again, work out what you can afford and get a mortgage offer before you find a home and make an offer.
- ❍ If you have a mortgage and think you might be able to get a better deal, find out whether your existing lender can help, then look around at other deals and work through the remortgaging calculator on page 76 to see if a switch is worth your while.

6 Protection

There are numerous protection policies on the market which will insure you against ill health, loss of income if you cannot work, or pay out a lump sum to your family if you die. You can insure yourself for care in your old age, and protect your possessions, your home and your car against damage or theft.

Everyone wants to feel their finances are secure and that their family is protected, but to take out all these insurances would cost hundreds of pounds each month. You need the cover which is suited to your needs, but no policy can cover you for every eventuality. So which ones should you avoid and which ones can't you do without? This section explains how all the different protection and security policies on the market work – and who they are suitable for.

What the State provides

When you are too ill to work:

- Weeks 1 to 28 of disability period, £55·70 a week for the employed and £47·10 for the self-employed.
- Weeks 29 to 52: incapacity benefit of £55·70.
- Week 53 onwards: £58·85.
- Other allowances payable relating to dependants.

There are medical tests to establish whether or not you are unfit to work – for the first 28 weeks this relates to your usual occupation, after that it relates to any work.

When someone dies:

- Widowed mother's allowance, up to £62·45 a week.
- Widow's pension, up to £62·45 a week.
- Widow's payment of £1,000.

A widow may also get any state earnings-related pension her husband had, but he must have paid enough National Insurance contributions (see Chapter 4)

Widowers, on the other hand, get non-means tested help only if they have children.

Protection checklist

Add up the amounts for income you would lose and extra costs you'd have to pay and deduct any income you'd gain or expenses you'd no longer have to pay. There are some suggestions of the sort of things to include on the left, but you should add those relevant to your own circumstances – it's a good idea to be as detailed as possible.

	DEATH		ILLNESS		REDUNDANCY	
	You £	Partner £	You £	Partner £	You £	Partner £
Income lost						
Earnings						
State benefits						
Pensions						
Other						
TOTAL 1						
Extra expenses						
Childcare						
Replace company car						
Other						
TOTAL 2						
Add totals 1 and 2 (A)						
Income gained						
State benefits						
Insurance						
New earnings						
Other						
TOTAL 3						
Expenses saved						
Travel to work						
Mortgage covered by insurance						
Other						
TOTAL 4						
Add totals 3 and 4 (B)						
Deduct (A) from (B)						

The box information on page 79 shows that help from the state is hardly substantial. Work through the protection checklist on the left to establish your protection priorities. Use the checklist to establish what your financial position would be were any of the following disasters to strike you or your spouse or partner: death, serious illness or disability (meaning you can't work or care for your family) or redundancy. If there is any shortfall, check whether you should plug the gap with insurance cover.

Life insurance

FIRST WE LOOK at the types of insurance which can help with these disasters: life insurance and health insurance.

If you have a family or people who depend on you, one of the most important types of insurance you can take out is life insurance – this pays out when you die. You can ensure that in such a time of crisis your family will at least not have to worry about money. It is important and available quite cheaply – so it's essential rather than luxury cover.

You may already have life insurance as some employers pay out three or four times your salary if you die in service. If your mortgage is backed by an endowment policy, it is likely that life cover will be built in to your policy and would pay off your mortgage if you died. Some critical illness insurances also include life cover (see page 83 for more details). It might also be provided under the terms of a personal pension plan. However, this will not be enough to support your family. To work out the amount of cover you need you should multiply your annual financial needs by 20, so, if you earn £25,000 a year you will need £500,000 worth of cover. This can be from a range of policies and could combine your employer's insurance, mortgage insurance and separate life insurance.

One of the cheapest ways to make sure you have extra cover is to take out term insurance (sometimes known as term assurance). This is simply life cover that you take out for a fixed term, say, 25 years. At the end of that time if you are still alive the policy ends and you get nothing back. There are several kinds of term insurance and, depending on what your circumstances are, one kind can be better than another. Apart from straightforward term insurance, which is useful if you are looking for life cover but want to put your savings elsewhere, there is:

- *Convertible term insurance*: You have the option to convert the policy to either a savings policy or whole-of-life policy. This can be suitable for people who later want the option of full life cover.
- *Whole-of-life insurance*: You are insured for your entire life, not just for an agreed term, and the policy will pay out when you die. Convertible and whole-of-life policies are usually more expensive than term insurance policies.
- *Renewable term insurance*: This allows you to extend the term of your policy when your agreed term is ended. If your health has deteriorated you will have to pay higher premiums.
- *Reviewable term insurance*: Your premiums are reviewed periodically to reflect the claiming patterns that have taken place. Because you share the risk with the insurance company initial premiums are often lower.
- *Family income benefit insurance*: This pays out an income to your family if you were to die during the agreed term of the policy. The income will be paid for the remainder of years left on the policy. So, if you were to die in the fifteenth year of a 20-year policy, your family would get an income for five years.

Cost

Although term insurance is one of the cheapest types of insurance on the market, premiums are affected by a number of factors:

Your age: The older you are the more you will pay for cover.

Your sex: Men pay more than women because they are more likely to die prematurely.

Your health: If you smoke or your health is poor you will pay more. If your condition is serious you might be refused cover.

Insurance term: The longer the policy term the more you will have to pay.

There are dozens of companies offering life insurance, and competition is fierce for your custom. It is therefore worth comparing a number of quotes before you decide on a policy. Once you have term insurance check your premiums against others on a regular basis. If you think you are paying too much, switch your policy. There are no penalties for doing so.

Do I need it?
Of all the insurances that you might consider taking out, term insurance is one of the most important, particularly when you have a family which depends on you financially. If you are single, term insurance isn't essential but if you have a mortgage you should make sure that you have cover to pay off the outstanding balance should you die prematurely.

It is probably worth looking only at life insurance rather than savings plan policies (such as endowment policies, unless they are attached to a mortgage). You would get a lump sum at the end of the term but they are not the cheapest way to get life cover. Also, if you have to cash in the policy early, although your life will still be insured, you may lose a lot of what you have invested in up-front charges. It is probably better to look at other ways of saving (see Chapters 8 and 9).

Health insurance

THERE ARE THREE MAIN TYPES of insurance which provide financial help when you are ill. They are:

- *Critical illness insurance*: This will pay out a lump sum if you are diagnosed as having a specific illness, such as cancer or a stroke.
- *Income replacement insurance*: This will pay out a proportion of your salary if you are unable to work because of sickness or accident.
- *Private medical insurance*: This will pay for your medical costs if you are ill.

CRITICAL ILLNESS INSURANCE

Critical illness cover pays out a cash lump sum if you are diagnosed as having one of a number of specified illnesses. The most usual illnesses to be covered are: cancer, coronary artery surgery, heart attack, kidney failure, a major organ transplant, multiple sclerosis, paralysis, or a stroke. Some policies may insure against conditions other than those mentioned here. And other policies will insure against additional conditions if you pay more towards the cost of the policy. There are two types of cover available:

- *Term cover*: This cover is usually an add-on policy, to your mortgage, for example. You are insured for a fixed number of years until the policy ends.
- *Whole-of-life cover:* You are insured for your entire life.

Benefits

If you are diagnosed as having one of the illnesses named on page 83, the policy will pay out a lump sum, which you can use for whatever you need. For example, you might need to pay for care if you cannot look after yourself, or extra medical costs. Alternatively, if your health is not badly affected, you could use the money to pay off your mortgage, or top up your pension plan. Most policies will cover you for total permanent disability and for diagnosis of a terminal illness, even if it is not listed above. You may have to live a certain amount of time (usually between 14 and 30 days, depending on the policy) before you are paid.

Your critical illness policy may also offer life cover. If you die during the period for which you are insured, the policy will pay out. You need to check, however, that if you claim for an illness your life cover is still intact because most policies won't pay out twice. If you have combined cover, it might be worth looking at getting a stand-alone life insurance policy, just in case you have to claim on the critical illness policy.

You can opt for a waiver of premium insurance. This means that your monthly contribution is paid during periods of illness.

You can take out guaranteed insurability so that you can increase your cover without having another health check after certain lifetime events, such as marriage, divorce, moving house or having a baby. Your children can be included in the cover. A typical policy will cover your children from the age of three to 18 for a range of listed illnesses. If your child has to claim, this will not affect a claim he or she makes in later life.

Independent financial adviser and *Moneywise* Ask The Professionals panellist Kean Seager says:

"Critical illness cover is a fairly recent development in the insurance industry. Initially premiums were quite expensive but it has become more and more popular and hence premiums have fallen significantly and can now represent good value. As we are all living longer our chances of contracting a critical illness have increased so it is well worth considering this type of cover."

Insurance costs

This is based on a couple both aged 50 next birthday. The male partner earns £25,000 a year in a medium-risk occupation and the couple live in a medium-risk area. Their mortgage costs £100 a month. If they were to take out the following policies, sample monthly premiums would add up to the following monthly insurance bill:

	Male	Female
Income replacement insurance *Scottish Amicable Income Protection (pays 75% income)*	£47·00	£69·75
Long-term care *PPP Lifetime Protection Plan (pays £1,000 a month)*	£48·27	£56·32
Mortgage payment protection *Halifax (costs £6·90 per £100)*	£3·45	£3·45
Private medical insurance *Norwich Union Express Care*	£77·49	£77·49
Monthly total	£176·21	£207·01

Drawbacks

If your condition takes a long time to diagnose, such as multiple sclerosis, you may have to wait a considerable time until you receive your benefit.

Some critical illness policies will pay out only if you contract the illness before you reach retirement age. If you become ill after you have retired you might have to wait until you are severely disabled before you are entitled to make a claim under the permanent disability option.

What won't you get cover for is HIV or AIDS. It is very difficult to find an insurer who will insure you for any AIDS-related condition but some may insure you for the symptoms of AIDS, such as kidney failure or some cancers. However, you won't be able to get insurance for those cancers which can have a high cure rate if they are caught early, such as skin cancer or testicular cancer.

Cost

The amount you pay for this insurance depends on several things.

Your age: The older you are, the more you will pay.

Your gender: Women pay less than men for cover and the difference becomes greater as you get older.

The state of your health: If you smoke or already have a health problem you will have to pay more.

Your occupation: If you have a risky occupation, you will pay more.

Whether you take out joint or single cover: It can be more cost effective for couples to take out cover jointly rather than independently.

Do I need it?

You may decide that your finances cannot stretch to critical illness cover and that you will make do with your savings and the benefits offered by other insurances, such as mortgage payment protection payment insurance, if you fall ill.

If you can afford cover, beware of taking out a cheap policy because it might have a high built-in growth assumption, which means that your premiums will rise as you get older. Look for policies with a lower-growth assumption or ones that have a built-in investment element. If you have to cash in your policy early, you won't get much in surrender value because of unit-linked investment charges and commission paid to advisers.

Find out what your employers will pay out if you fall sick. They may continue to pay your salary for a limited period of, say, six months and if you are severely disabled and cannot return to work you might be able to draw your employers pension early.

Income replacement insurance

An alternative to critical illness insurance is income replacement insurance (otherwise known as permanent health insurance). This kicks in if you cannot work because of illness or accident and will pay you 65–75% of your salary until you return to work or until the age at which you have chosen for your benefits to stop. This could be your normal retirement age. Some employers offer income replacement insurance as a perk (check with the personnel department). There are three types of cover available:

- *Own occupation cover*: This insures you if you are not able to continue in your own occupation. This is usually the most expensive insurance. If you are regarded by the insurance company as being a higher-than-average risk you may not be able to get own occupation cover.
- *Any suitable occupation cover*: If you are unable to do any work for which you are qualified or have an aptitude.
- *Any occupation cover*: If you are unable to return to any kind of work. This is usually the cheapest cover.

Benefits

If you are unable to work you can get up to 75% of your salary until your normal retirement age. With critical illness you might get a £100,000 lump sum payout but that is only worth five years' salary at £20,000 at today's rates. Imagine what would happen if you fell ill at 35 and could no longer work? The range of illnesses covered is much wider and you can also claim income replacement insurance if you have an accident and are unable to return to work. You can opt for:

Cover for a partner or spouse: This is applicable to anyone who stays at home to look after children or an elderly person.

Unemployment cover: Insurance if you fall ill when out of work.

Relapse benefit: You won't have to wait for another deferment period if you fall ill with the same condition again.

Partial benefit: You will get a reduced pay-out if you are able to return to work part-time or have to take a lower paid job.

Waiver of premium benefit: You don't have to pay any premiums if you are claiming benefit.

Drawbacks

You can't claim income replacement insurance immediately. This is not a policy which will pay out if you have a short-term illness so there is a deferment period of at least one month, and up to a year, before you receive payment. There is an advantage in that if you choose a long deferment period your premiums will be cheaper. You won't get disablement caused by:

- Alcohol or drug abuse.
- HIV and/or AIDS-related conditions.
- War.
- Pregnancy.

- Self-inflicted injury.
- Pre-existing medical conditions.
- Failure to seek or follow medical advice.

Cost

As with critical illness, what you pay depends on certain factors:

Your age: The older you are the more you pay.

Your sex: Premiums tend to be higher for women than men.

Your occupation: If you do a risky job, you may be refused cover. Risky occupations might include jobs in the armed forces, building labourers and refuse collection, for example.

The deferment period: If you can wait a long time before your benefit is paid, your premiums will be lower.

Your retirement date: If you choose an early retirement date your premiums will be lower.

Depending on which policy you choose, your premiums will increase in different ways. There are four main types of premium:

Guaranteed: Your premium will not go up unless you choose an increasing benefit option.

Reviewable: Your premiums may increase following a review of your status. Reviews vary from an annual one for the first five years to one review after five years.

Unit-linked: Your premiums will paid into a unit-linked investment fund and if the fund underperforms your premiums will increase to compensate for the shortfall.

With-profits: Your premiums will be higher than the other policies above but you can expect a good return when the policy matures. These policies are usually offered through Friendly Societies.

Do I need it?

If you are self-employed, this is one insurance you should definitely think about because you have no employer to pay sick pay if you don't work.

If you are employed, find out what your employer's sick-pay scheme offers before you take out this insurance. It could be that you will get your full salary for a limited period and can take your employers pension early if you cannot work again.

This insurance can be expensive and if you don't make a claim you won't see anything at maturity unless you choose a with-profits policy. You may have to go through rigorous examination before you can satisfy insurers that you have a claim and they will make regular follow-up checks.

Private medical insurance

Private medical insurance (PMI) will pay the cost of medical treatment if you want private care and need to see a doctor or spend time in hospital. You will either stay in an NHS hospital in a private ward, or in a private hospital.

This is one insurance which is not essential if you are happy with the care that you receive with the NHS. You should also remember that private medical insurance will not cover you for every medical mishap. If you break your finger, for example, and need out-patient treatment you will probably have to seek NHS treatment, while some long-term chronic illnesses, such as arthritis or asthma, will not be covered under private medical policies. Pregnancy care and GP services are also normally excluded. If you want to avoid NHS waiting lists for treatment and you like the idea of hotel-style accommodation when you are in hospital then PMI might be for you. Check before you take out PMI whether your employer offers it as a perk.

There are three types of cover available:

- *Top-level cover*: This is the most expensive and offers the most comprehensive level of cover. You will have a greater number of hospitals to choose from and hotel-style accommodation. Depending on where you live, and particularly if you live in a big city with a famous teaching hospital, you might have to choose this band if the policy you go for selects cover by region.
- *Medium-level cover*: This type of cover is not so comprehensive as top-level cover but offers more than budget-level cover.
- *Budget-level cover*: This offers fewer frills; you won't have so many hospitals to choose from and your dinner menu may be less exciting but you should still get a good range of cover. Many people choose this level of cover, especially if their policies allow them to upgrade to a higher level if they need it.

Benefits

You shouldn't have to wait so long for care and you can get faster access to a specialist. If you choose top-level cover, you will be covered for the following. Budget-level cover will cover you for most of these things:

- Out-patient consultations and treatment, and day-care surgery when you don't need to stay overnight.
- In-patient treatment, such as nursing, specialists' fees, drugs or physiotherapy.
- The costs of an operation, including surgeons and anaesthetists' fees.
- A cash sum if you receive NHS treatment. This can be around £100 a night.
- An out-of-band benefit If the treatment you need is in a higher band hospital, the policy will cover it.

Typical extra benefits include the following:

- Nursing care if you need care at home.
- The use of a private ambulance.
- Referral to a practitioner who specialises in alternative medicine.
- Cover for staying with your child overnight if he or she is sick.

You might also be entitled to a cash payment if you have a baby.

Some policies offer overseas cover so that your medical and repatriation costs will be covered if you fall ill abroad.

Drawbacks

The problem with PMI is that it won't cover you for everything and there will be times when you will still receive NHS care. If you are a young, healthy woman for example, you will not get any private pregnancy or childbirth care under the terms of most policies. The cover also imposes limits on treatment. One of the most common is a restriction on out-patient treatment that isn't linked to a course of treatment, such as for a broken finger. Medical insurance isn't regulated in the same way as other investment products, so check that your insurer is a member of the Insurance Ombudsman Scheme.

What you won't get cover for: You won't be able to claim for medical treatment for long-term illnesses, such as asthma, arthritis or terminal cancer, although some treatable cancers might be included.

If you have a pre-existing illness of any kind you won't get cover even though you might not be aware of the illness. Any Conditions relating to a pre-existing illness will also be excluded although you might be able to get cover if you are willing to pay higher premiums.

Other exclusions are:

- Injuries from sport or attempted suicide.
- Treatment for AIDS related conditions.
- Alcoholism or substance abuse.
- Pregnancy, childbirth and fertility treatment.
- Dental and optical treatment.
- Psychiatric treatment.
- Cosmetic surgery.
- GP services.

Cost

The amount you pay will depend on your age, your state of health and the level of cover you choose. Premiums will increase as you grow older and medical costs also rise. Some insurers charge by region, so if you live in an area with top-band hospitals you may not have much choice over the cover you can choose. Insurers can give you a list of how they rate hospitals before you decide on cover. Some insurers charge a flat rate, so you won't have to worry about which hospital to choose. Most offer out-of-band cover so that you will be entitled to treatment in a higher-rated hospital if you need it. Most plans will let you choose an excess to help keep your premiums down. Excesses are usually between £100 and £250, which means that if you have to make a claim, you will pay this amount before the insurance takes over. With some policies you can choose up to 50% of your premium as an excess, which could allow you to go for a higher level of cover than you could normally afford. Some policies offer a no-claims discount so that your premiums will be cheaper if you stay healthy. If you are over 60 you no longer get tax relief of 23% on your premiums.

> Independent financial adviser and *Moneywise* Ask The Professionals panellist Kean Seager says:
>
> "Private medical insurance can be very useful for minor problems and where you would like to be dealt with quickly and at your own convenience. It can also suit people who like to spend money to stay in a swanky hotel rather than a B&B."

How do I make a claim?

As soon as you become ill or you are referred by your GP for specialist treatment, you should inform your insurer because your illness may not be covered under the policy terms.

So do I need it?
If you are happy with treatment under the NHS, you don't need PMI. Alternatively, your employer might offer it as a perk but you will pay tax on the contributions. If you are self-employed it can be worth considering as you may have more control over when you receive treatment. Premiums may be prohibitively expensive for older people and the chronically and long-term sick will probably have to return to NHS care. If you are concerned about NHS waiting lists, you could go for a budget plan.

Hospital cash plans

Hospital cash plans are a well-established way of paying for healthcare if you need it. Usually run by small local associations, they pre-date many private medical schemes on offer today. The cover they offer is usually more limited than that offered by private medical insurance and depends on your monthly premiums.

If you claim on the policy you usually get a fixed cash payment for every night you spend in hospital. This could be £100 a week or £100 a night if you have paid top premiums. This amount could help towards the cost of treatment if you opt for private treatment, or cover some of your lost earnings if you have NHS care, whichever is more appropriate. You may also get help towards the cost of optical and dental care, a maternity benefit, physiotherapy and convalescent care or outpatient treatment. You may even get a cash payment when you have a baby. You usually have to be insured for a minimum period, say six to 12 months, before you qualify for all the benefits on offer.

You can take out a hospital cash plan as a stand-alone policy or as an add-on to another private medical insurance plan. Check if your insurer offers this facility.

Is it worth it?
Hospital cash plans look like good value at first glance but there are a few things to bear in mind before you sign up. Most of them do not offer the comprehensive cover that you would get with a medical insurance plan and if breadth of cover is a concern for you, then you would be better off taking out a dedicated medical insurance plan. You would have to pay fairly high premiums anyway to get a fairly decent level of cover, so private medical insurance would not be much more expensive.

If you are happy with NHS treatment and would welcome a cash boost if you were to go into hospital or you would like help with the cost for services, such as optical and dental treatment, which are not automatically available with many private medical insurance plans, then hospital cash plans may be worth looking at.

Long-term care insurance

Even if you spend all your working life fit and healthy and never spend time off work because of illness, the situation can change when you get older. Many people are concerned about who will care for them if they can no longer look after for themselves. Families now live further apart and you may not be able to rely on them to be there all the time. Alternatively, you might not want to place the burden of your care on to another family member.

Until recently, you could expect comprehensive state help if you had to receive long-term nursing care in your old age. But changes to the law in 1993 meant that people with assets of over £8,000 had to pay all the costs of their care. As residential and nursing care costs on average between £300 and £500 a week, lifetime savings could be eaten away in a very short time. Amendments to the law have raised the threshold at which state help ends to £16,000 but as most people own property, which counts as an asset, only a few are still entitled to free care.

Insurance companies have been quick to spot that people resent handing over their assets to the State to fund their care, and have developed long-term care insurance policies designed to meet the costs of care if you need it without eating into your capital. This insurance has been slow to take off, partly because it is expensive and partly because people have been waiting to see whether a Labour government would back-track on current funding and restore it to previous levels. But with annual care costs estimated at £42 billion, and an ageing population, this is unlikely to happen. Labour has promised to look at ways to fund long-term care but its report may not appear until 1999.

Long-term care insurance is supposed to plug the gap between what the state will provide and what you will have to pay if you need nursing or residential care. The insurance kicks in if you are unable to look after yourself. This is assessed by how many Activities of Daily Living (ADLs) you can perform. The section below lists what they are. If you fail a certain number of activities, usually between two or three, the policy will pay out. Before you can claim you may also be tested for cognitive impairment, that is illnesses which affect your mental ability, such as Alzheimer's disease. The maximum benefit you will receive depends on how much you are insured for, but it usually has a ceiling of £30,000 a year.

Activities of daily living (ADLs)

A list of everyday activities you need to carry out yourself to maintain a minimum level of sustenance and hygiene. These include:

- Washing.
- Dressing.
- Feeding.
- Toileting.
- Mobility.
- Continence.

Most companies will quote five or six ADLs and you need to fail two or three of these activities before you can claim on the policy.

There are three ways to pay for care. If you want to pay for care in advance you can do so in two ways:

- Through a monthly contribution plan.
- By putting in a single premium which is invested and then grows to provide income. You won't get this back if you survive for more than five years.

If you want to pay for care now:

- You can take out an immediate plan. You invest a lump sum which gives you an income to pay for your care. You will get a higher income if your life expectancy is shorter.
- You can buy it as an add-on to another type of insurance policy.

Benefits

You do not place the burden of care on your family. You may not have to use up your capital assets so you will have more money to leave to your family. You can elect to be cared for in your own home. You may get financial help with special equipment to make your everyday life easier if you stay at home.

You can take out joint cover, and most companies will offer a discount of 10% to 20% on premiums. Some companies may offer care to the second partner only, on the assumption that if one partner remains fit and healthy, he or she will look after the other.

Drawbacks

This insurance is expensive and premiums rise as you get older. The assessment of ADLs is very strict. If you can achieve the tasks with special equipment or with the help of someone else, you may not be able to claim. You might have to be severely disabled or impaired before you can get access to care. The insurance will not pay out if you need to go into a nursing home for a short period to give your partner or family member a break from looking after you.

You might never need the insurance. According to Age Concern, only one person in 20 under the age of 85 needs specialist care, although this figure rises to one in four after the age of 85. At 60, men can expect to live another 18·2 years and women another 22·2 years.

Cost

The premiums you pay are affected by different factors:

Your age: If you opt for the monthly payment policies premiums will rise as you get older and the risk of you needing care gets greater. However, with lump-sum premiums costs rise very little between ages 50 and 70 because the premium has a built-in increase in cover.

Your gender: Women usually pay more than men because they generally live longer. At current rates, a 50-year-old man would need to pay a lump sum of about £12,000 to get £12,000 a year worth of cover. A woman of the same age would have to pay almost £23,000 to get £12,000 a year.

Your health: You will pay more if you are already in poor health but with a non life-threatening condition. If your life expectancy is short, you may get a better deal.

Deferment periods: If your policy has a long built-in deferment period you might pay less. Minimum deferment is usually four weeks but you can wait up to 26 weeks before you receive care.

Increases in costs: Nursing home fees are likely to continue to rise, so you will need to build in an annual increase to ensure that your costs will be met if you need to claim.

Limiting care: You can reduce your premiums if you opt to put a limit on the number of years' care you will receive. The average length of stay in a nursing home is two years, so you could limit care to five years. It is worth having back-up funds, though, in case you survive for longer.

Independent financial adviser and *Moneywise* Ask The Professionals panellist Kean Seager says:

"Some people hand over the ownership of their house to their children. This can seem quite sensible but there are pitfalls. For example, it is not unknown for families to fall out and this can lead to genuine difficulties. Similarly, if one of your children ends up getting divorced your house would be regarded as one of their assets to be split between them. Broadly speaking, I am rather against this manoeuvre although it can work out quite well in certain circumstances."

Do I need it?

Long-term care insurance can be useful if you have no one to look after you in your old age but remember that only one in 20 people under the age of 85 ends up needing specialist care. If you don't need the care you are unlikely to get anything back if you don't make a claim, and costs are expensive.

If you worry that you might need care in old age and have the time to invest it might be better to set up your own contingency plan by investing a lump sum or setting up a regular savings plan. If you wrap the investment in a personal equity plan (PEP), the income on it will be tax free. That way, if you never have to pay for care, you will be able to use the savings for something else.

Handing over your house to a relative may seem like a good idea but if you need to go into a residential home and the Local Authority which assesses your needs can prove that you did it to avoid having to pay for care, it may include your home's value as a notional asset.

You also have to assess how you feel about someone else owning your home, however good the relationship is now. If you never fall ill, a home can be sold to release extra capital to fund your retirement. If you relinquish control you may not be able to make these decisions independently.

The handover rules for tax purposes are also complicated. If the total value of your estate comes to more than £215,000 (at 1997/98 rates), you have to survive for seven years in order for your house to be free from inheritance tax (IHT). If you die within that time, your heirs will be charged IHT on a sliding scale. However, if you continue to live in the house the seven years will not start running until you move out. While you continue to live there, if you pay a full rent to the relative you've handed your home to, it won't be included in your estate. But your relative would probably have to pay tax on the rental income.

Once you have protected yourself and your family, look at protecting your home and possessions. Some of these insurances are essential if you don't have some of the policies above; others are just essential.

Credit insurance

THIS INSURANCE WILL normally be offered to you when you take out a mortgage, a loan or credit card. It is designed to protect your payments if you are sick, have an accident or are made redundant. The cover is usually limited to 12 months.

MORTGAGE PAYMENT PROTECTION

Changes to state benefits in 1995 mean that if you take out a new mortgage now and are subsequently made redundant or cannot work because of illness, you will have to wait 39 weeks from the start of your claim before you are entitled to help with mortgage interest payments from the state. Even if you had a mortgage before 1 October 1995 and you are unable to work, you will get nothing for eight weeks and only half of your costs paid for the next 18 weeks, after which all your costs will be paid.

How much does it cost?

The cost is usually worked out on each £100 of your mortgage payments and ranges between £5 and £7 per month. So, if your mortgage payments are £400 per month, cover will cost between £20 and £28 per month.

Is it worth taking out?

If you are seriously worried about losing your job it might be worth considering but you cannot rely on just this insurance alone. Most policies have an excess of up to 90 days before they pay out, so you will already need to have some savings to cover this period.

There are also a lot of exclusions: it may be hard to get cover if you are self-employed, a new employee, on a short-term contract, or over 60.

If you decide to take out mortgage payment protection, look for a policy with few exclusions and a short excess period. Don't look on it as the answer to your mortgage problems if you can't work.

OTHER LOANS

The cover offered can be costly. For example, on a £1,000 loan repayable over a year with Lloyds Bank the monthly repayments are £91.40 without insurance and £99.19 with insurance. Loan protection schemes on credit cards cost around 70p a month.

Other ways to protect your finances

INSURANCE ISN'T NECESSARILY the answer to all the problems you fear will leave you with financial troubles. And there are specific options with insurance you need to look out for.

- If you fear redundancy, loan protection insurances are worth considering but shop around to get the best deal.
- If you fear illness, critical illness insurance or permanent health insurance would provide a lump sum or income to help you cope financially so you won't need payment protection.
- Create an advance position by saving up at least three months' mortgage payments or by paying off three months' payments in advance.
- Take out waiver of premium options on pensions or life insurances so that your payments will be protected.
- Keep money in a flexible savings plan so that you won't be penalised if you have to stop payments and you can get at the money if you need it. This includes some TESSAs and PEPs, as well as instant access building society accounts.

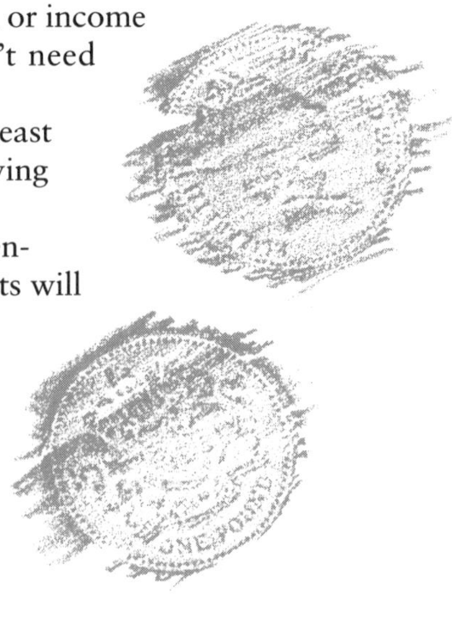

Home and motor insurance

THESE ARE ESSENTIAL types of insurance. In fact, it is illegal not to have motor insurance. The market for these insurances is fierce and it is one area where it pays to shop around before you take out a policy.

HOME INSURANCE

- *Buildings insurance*: This covers the amount it would cost to rebuild your home and other buildings, such as a garage, as well as driveways and fixtures and fittings, such as kitchens and bathrooms. You would also be covered for the cost of alternative accommodation while your home was being rebuilt or repaired.

  Rebuilding costs are generally lower than the market value so you should always keep an eye on house prices to make sure you are not under-insured. The Rebuilding Costs Calculator on page 100 shows how you can work out how much cover you need if your house is of standard construction.
- *Contents insurance*: There are two ways to assess cover:
  A sum-insured policy: You add up the total replacement cost of all your possessions and insure yourself for that amount.
  A room-rated policy: Cover is calculated on the number of bedrooms or habitable rooms in your home. You don't have to work out the value of your possessions but you could end up with too much cover unless you have a lot of possessions.

Most contents policies will also cover accidental damage to possessions and items temporarily away from the home as well as the theft of credit cards and money.

Cost

Most insurers will start with a basic premium, which is calculated according to where you live and the amount you want to insure. Your premium may then be discounted according to several factors:

- Your age.
- How secure your home is.
- Your claims record. You might build up a no-claims discount.
- How much excess you want to pay. The higher the excess the greater the discount.
- Whether someone is at home during the day. If there is someone at home during the day, premiums will be cheaper.

How to work out the buildings insurance cover you need

1. Work out the total external size of your property in square feet. Double this figure for a two-storey property. If your house has a third storey, only three-quarters of the area of the third storey need be added to the total. An integral garage should also be included in the calculation.
2. Using the 'Cost of rebuilding' table (opposite), identify your type of house and the region it is in, then look up the rebuilding costs per square foot. The figures in the table are based on properties of an average quality finish so, if your home has a luxury kitchen or bathroom or double-glazed windows, you may have to add up to 25% on to the total cost of rebuilding.
3. If you have a separate or built-on garage, add on the cost of rebuilding this. The costs can range from £2,950 for a single pre-fabricated garage to £8,700 for a double detached garage in brick. You will then need to add an allowance for fences, walls and sheds.

Rebuilding costs calculator
Use the following table to calculate how much your home is worth.

	Your home	Example
Total area of property in sq ft		1,650 sq ft
Rebuilding cost per sq ft (from 'Cost of rebuilding' table opposite)		£74·50
Multiply area by cost per sq ft		£104,300
Add an amount for better than average:		
decoration		£1,500
bathroom suite		£1,350
cloakroom suite		–
fitted kitchen		£1,700
double glazing		–
Add cost of rebuilding:		
garage		£2,950
garden walls		£300
fences		£200
patio		£350
greenhouse		–
shed		£400
swimming pool		–
tennis court		–
Sub total		£113,050
Add an allowance for inflation @ 5% if your policy is not index-linked		£5,653
Total		**£118,703**

Continued on opposite page

The cost of rebuilding

This table helps you to identify your type of home, the region it's in, and the rebuilding costs per square foot. The figures are January 1997 costings, per square foot of the external floor area.

	Region	1920-1945 Large/Medium/Small	1946-1979 Large/Medium/Small	1980-present Large/Medium/Small
Detached house	1	£70·50/£74·50/£76·00	£59·00/£63·50/£65·50	£57·50/£57·50/£51·50
	2	£64·50/£67·50/£69·50	£59·50/£58·00/£59·50	£52·50/£52·50/£56·00
	3	£60·00/£63·00/£64·50	£49·50/£54·00/£55·50	£49·00/£48·50/£52·00
	4	£57·00/£60·00/£61·50	£47·50/£51·50/£53·00	£48·50/£45·50/£50·00
Typical area ft^2		2,550/1,350/1,050 ft^2	2,550/1,350/1,050 ft^2	2,400/1,400/950 ft^2
Semi-detached house	1	£78·50/£74·00/£74·00	£55·50/£58·50/£62·5	£60·50/£61·00/£65·50
	2	£69·50/£67·00/£67·5	£50·50/£53·00/£56·5	£55·00/£58·50/£59·50
	3	£61·50/£59·50/£59·5	£44·50/£47·00/£50·5	£48·50/£49·00/£53·00
	4	£62·00/£60·00/£60·0	£45·00/£47·50/£50·5	£49·00/£49·00/£53·00
Typical area ft^2		1,350/1,150/900 ft^2	1,650/1,350/1,050 ft^2	1,600/900/650 ft^2
Detached bungalow	1	£74·50/£69·00/£71·5	£63·00/£63·50/£66·5	£64.50/£65.00/£67·00
	2	£67·50/£63·00/£65·0	£57·00/£58·00/£60·5	£58.50/£59.00/£61·00
	3	£63·00/£58·50/£60·5	£53·00/£54·00/£56·5	£54.50/£55.00/£56.50
	4	£60·00/£56·00/£58·0	£51·00/£51·50/£54·0	£52.00/£52·50/£54.00
Typical area ft^2		1,650/1,400/1,000 ft^2	2,500/1,350/1,000 ft^2	1,900/950/750 ft^2
Semi-detached bungalow	1	£76·00/£73·50/£71·0	£60·00/£61·50/£66·0	£62.50/£70.00/£73·50
	2	£69·00/£66·50/£64·5	£54·50/£58·00/£60·0	£58.50/£63.50/£66·50
	3	£64·00/£62·00/£60·0	£50·50/£52·00/£56·0	£52.50/£59.00/£62·00
	4	£61·50/£59·50/£57·5	£48·50/£49·50/£53·5	£50.50/£56.50/£59·50
Typical area ft^2		1,350/1,200/800 ft^2	1,350/1,200/800 ft^2	950/550/500 ft^2
Terraced house	1	£76·50/£76·50/£76·0	£55·00/£60·00/£66·5	£62.00/£64·00/£63.50
	2	£69·50/£69·50/£69·0	£46·50/£50·00/£54·5	£56·50/£58.00/£58.00
	3	£65·00/£65·00/£61·0	£44·50/£50·50/£56·0	£52·50/£54·00/£54·00
	4	£62·00/£62·00/£61·5	£44·50/£48·50/£53·5	£50·50/£51·50/£51·50
Typical area ft^2		1,350/1,050/850 ft^2	1,650/1,300/900 ft^2	900/750/650 ft^2

Regions

1 London Boroughs and Channel Islands (building costs in the Channel Islands are affected by local conditions and may vary from prices in this band – you should seek local advice). **2** Scotland and the South East (Bedfordshire, Berkshire, Buckinghamshire, Essex, Hampshire, Hertfordshire, Kent, Oxfordshire, Surrey, East Sussex, West Sussex).North West **3** East Anglia, Northern,South West, and Yorkshire and Humberside. **4** East Midlands, West Midlands, Wales, and Northern Ireland (building costs in Northern Ireland are considerably lower than in the rest of the UK and may be 20% below the costs given for Region 4).

Figures for houses built before 1920 are also available from the ABI on 0171 600 3333.

Before you buy

Work out how much cover you need. Find out what you will be covered for. Expensive paintings or jewellery might need to be covered separately. Ask about discounts. Get as many quotes you can. If you are a member of a professional body or trade union, it might offer cheaper insurance.

MOTOR INSURANCE

If you own a car, you are required by law to have motor insurance. This covers you if you injure someone else or another car or property while you are driving. There are three types of insurance:

- *Third party*: This covers you against injury to someone else, another car or property. It is the minimum level of cover.
- *Third party, fire and theft*: This covers you for the above and for possible fire in or theft of your car.
- *Comprehensive cover*: This covers you for all the above plus accidental damage to your car, personal accident, medical expenses, loss or damage to personal effects in your car, including stereos, although sometimes you pay extra for this. You might also get a temporary car if your own has to be repaired, while some insurers will pay for the cost of overnight accommodation if you are stranded away from home. If your car is less than a year old and is written off your insurer might replace it or give you cash towards a new one. You will also be covered if you drive someone else's car but this may be limited to third-party cover.

Cost

This is set according to a number of factors:

Your age: The younger you are the more you will pay.

Your job: Some occupations are seen as being a higher risk than others, so you will pay more.

Where you live: There are more claims in urban areas, so if you live in a town you'll pay more than if you live in the country.

Your driving history: If you have had any accidents or have points on your licence you will pay more. Women and older drivers are generally seen as a lower risk.

The premium you start out paying will reduce if you don't make any claims and you will be entitled to a No Claims Discount (NCD). Discounts vary but they can make an enormous difference to your premiums. After one year of claim-free motoring you might get a discount of around 30% rising to 60% if you do not make a claim over the next five or six years.

Your NCD is therefore very valuable and you can protect it if you are under 25 or over 60. This can cost between 10% and 20% of the premium. However, you won't be able to make many claims before your premiums start to rise again and you lose your discount. If your car is stolen or you damage it you may lose your NCD. To protect it, you can pay for damage repairs yourself if you can afford them. If you decide to change insurers you can usually take your NCD with you. You may not qualify for a NCD if you have been driving on someone else's insurance, living abroad or driving a company car, but most insurers offer an introductory discount for over 25s who have a history of claim-free motoring.

Before you buy

Get a range of quotes. The competition for your custom is fierce. Make sure you know what you are covered for. If you are willing to pay an excess, premiums may be cheaper. Find out if your professional body or trade union offers discounted insurance.

Action plan

- ❍ Work through the protection checklist on page 80 to establish how your death or illness would affect your family's finances.
- ❍ Check 'What the State provides' on page 79 to see how a disaster would affect your financial position.
- ❍ If you don't have any life insurance but you do have dependants, this is a priority. You can get a policy which pays out a lump sum or income.
- ❍ Look at the benefits provided by critical illness insurance and income replacement insurance to see which is most appropriate. If you are self-employed you should take out income replacement insurance.
- ❍ If you are not happy with the care available on the NHS, check out private medical insurance.
- ❍ Think about how you would pay if you had to be cared for in your old age – start some savings or look into long-term care insurance.
- ❍ When your house or car insurance comes up for renewal, don't automatically continue with the same insurer – shop around for the best deal.

7 Planning your retirement

This chapter is relevant to everyone. You might think you're too young to start thinking about retirement, but you need to get some pension arrangements in place in your twenties, to ensure you'll be able to retire in comfort. Everyone over 30 should have some financial plans arranged for retirement.

Retirement planning is all about starting early and contributing regularly towards your pension fund. You're not taxed on the income you contribute to a pension, which makes pensions an efficient ways to save for your retirement. Even if you start off with modest contributions the longer they are invested the more time they will have to grow. As your needs change and your expenses decrease, you will be able to contribute more.

Pensions often offer more than just your retirement income. You might also get:

- Built-in life insurance.
- A tax-free lump sum when you retire.
- Pensions for your widowed spouse if you die before retirement.
- A reduced pension for your widowed spouse if you die after you retire.
- A reduced pension for dependent children if you die.

Pensions should form the basis of your retirement planning – but it is a good idea to supplement them with some long-term savings and investments(see Chapter 10, page 189).

There is lots going on in the world of pensions so it's worth keeping up to date with any new developments. In July 1997 the government announced that it was conducting a pensions review which should be completed by April 1998. It is likely that a new form of 'stakeholder pension' will be offered – and some argue that it may become compulsory to contribute to a private pension. The new system may offer opportunities for pension planning to people with broken career patterns or on low incomes. Also in July 1997, the

Office of Fair Trading suggested that a new type of 'designated pension' linked to funds which track the stockmarket should be introduced.

Pensions also received a blow in the last Budget which means you may need to boost any pensions you already have in place. Pension funds are not liable to tax themselves. However, this tax break was severely curtailed in the July 1997 Budget. Chancellor Gordon Brown abolished pension funds' right to reclaim tax paid on dividends from investments in shares. As pension funds have large stockmarket holdings this will have a big impact on their capacity for growth. Exactly how this will affect your options is not yet clear – it will depend on what your pension plan provider decides to do. It could be worth getting in touch to find out what its plans are. This means it's even more important to start a pension early or to assess how your pension is doing. You may find you'll need to make extra contributions. The Inland Revenue limits the amount of contributions you can make – if you're up to the limit, you might need to use other investments to make extra provision.

Your income in retirement

THE FIRST STEP, whatever your age and whether or not you're in a pension, is to work out what income you'll want in retirement.You'll then be able to see whether your arrangements are on target or whether you need to set things up.

RETIREMENT CALCULATOR

Part One: Your essential monthly outgoings in retirement

Remember that some of these costs will be lower when you retire so put in an estimate of the lower cost. Some – heating and light – may increase, so put in a higher estimate than your current bills (see table opposite).

Part Two: Other non-essential outgoings

These are the 'quality of life' things, not just the ordinary household expenses. This section should include the cost of hobbies and holidays in retirement. Try and estimate a monthly cost for this category (see table on page 108).

	Estimated monthly outgoings	Example
Grocery shopping (food, cleaning, toiletries, etc)		£250
Rent or mortgage payments		–
Council tax		£60
Gas and electricity		£60
Phone bill		£25
Running costs of car (tax, petrol, insurance, AA/RAC membership)		£100
Other transport costs		£10
Clothing and shoes		£40
Dry cleaning, laundry		£5
Hairdresser		£25
Home maintenance (cleaning, window cleaner, gardening, repairs)		£30
Home and buildings insurance		£60
Life insurance and endowment policies		–
Other regular savings		–
Hire purchase or loan payments		£25
Other		£25
Total monthly outgoings		**£715**

This will give you an idea of the amount of income you're likely to need in retirement. Of course this is in today's values. The table on the next page below shows how inflation at different rates erodes spending power and so you need to boost your estimate to get a better idea of what you should be aiming at. Although this will still be a fairly rough estimate, it will give you something to work towards.

	Estimated monthly cost	Example
Holidays		£120
Eating out		£60
Theatre and cinema, etc		£30
Newspapers and magazines		£25
Drink		£50
Tobacco		–
Spending on pets		£25
Spending on the garden		£25
Birthday and Christmas presents		£20
The cost of hobbies		£20
Monthly savings for an emergency fund (to buy a car, put in a downstairs bathroom, etc)		£40
Total 'non-essential' outgoings		**£415**
Total outgoings (sum of Parts One and Two)		**£1,130**
Annual outgoings (12 x the figure above)		**£13,560**

The effects of inflation

This table shows the buying power of £1,000 in future at different rates of inflation

Inflation	5 years	10 years	15 years	20 years
2·5%	£884	£781	£690	£610
5%	£784	£614	£481	£377
7·5%	£697	£485	£338	£235
10%	£621	£386	£239	£149

Source: The Annuity Bureau

State pensions

FIRST WE TAKE A LOOK at what you can expect from the State in the form of income in your retirement. There are three different types of state pension.

Independent financial adviser and *Moneywise* Ask The Professionals panellist Rebekah Kearey says:

"The state pension system has been altered regularly ever since it began in 1948 because the cost to provide for the State's pensioners in the manner that was intended has proved too expensive to maintain."

BASIC STATE PENSION

To qualify for the Basic State Pension, you need to have made sufficient National Insurance contributions. This tax year (1997/98) assuming you have made all your National Insurance contributions, the full basic pension for a single person is £62·45 a week (£3,247·40 a year).

A married woman can qualify for the relevant amount of the single person's pension if she has made enough National Insurance contributions. If both partners have made full contributions they will get £6,494·80 a year. If a married woman hasn't made full National Insurance contributions she would receive a pension based on her husband's National Insurance contribution record. Currently the joint pension is £99·80 a week (£5,189·60 a year). Pension rates rise in line with inflation every year from April and each pensioner also receives a £10 Christmas bonus.

State pensions are already low and there is no prospect of this position improving, so you cannot rely on them. If your employer offers a pension scheme this is probably your best bet. Otherwise, or if you're self-employed, you need a personal pension.

The statutory retirement age in the UK is currently 65 for men and 60 for women but it is due to be set at an equal age of 65 for both men and women. If you are a woman who was born after 6 April 1950 but before 5 March 1955 you will fall under the transitional arrangements and your retirement age will be set according to your birth date and fall between 60 and 65. To work out when you can retire, count the whole months after 6 April 1950 which fall after your 60th birthday. This will be your retirement date. Women born after 6 March 1955 will be able to retire at 65.

To qualify for a state pension you need to have made National Insurance contributions for at least a quarter of your working life. Your working life is defined as the tax year in which your 16th birthday falls through to the last full tax year before you reach state pension age, which is currently 65 for men and 60 for women. If you manage to contribute for nine-tenths of your working life (44 years) you will get the full state pension. Most people, however, don't manage this but if you have made contributions for at least a quarter of your working life you will get a reduced pension.

Although you pay contributions from your salary, there are circumstances when you are unable to work. In some cases you will receive National Insurance credits. These are when:

- You are still in full-time education between 16 and 18.
- You are on an approved training course (not university).
- You are claiming benefits such as unemployment benefit, maternity benefit or incapacity benefit.
- You are an unemployed man aged between 60 and 65.

If you are at home because you are looking after children or an elderly relative you qualify for home responsibilities protection. This reduces the total number of years you need to make National Insurance contributions to qualify for a state pension. You automatically receive the protection if you are claiming child benefit but if you are looking after an elderly person you will need to notify your local Benefits Agency. The address will be in your local phone book.

You won't be building up a pension if you are at university, taking a career break or living abroad, but you can make up for the lost years by paying Class 3 National Insurance contributions, which are currently £6·05 a week for the 1997/98 tax year. You are allowed to fill in any gaps in your National Insurance record for the last six years.

There are four classes of National Insurance:

- Class 1 is paid by both employees and employers.
- Class 2 is paid by the self-employed.
- Class 3 is a voluntary payment which you pay when you want to plug the gaps in your record because you weren't making any contributions.
- Class 4 is paid by the self-employed and is a tax. Its contributions do not go towards pensions or state benefits.

State Earnings Related Pension Scheme (SERPS)

This is a pension scheme available to employees only. How much you get at the end of your working life with a SERPS pension depends on your earnings and for how long you contributed. It can be very valuable and almost double your state pension if you have paid in enough.

You can only build up a SERPS pension if you are paying Class 1 contributions and earn more than £61 a week, which is the threshold for paying National Insurance. You can 'contract out' of SERPS if you are a member of a suitable employers pension scheme or if you have a personal pension set up for the purpose of receiving the SERPS pension contributions.

Contracting out means that you don't pay into the SERPS pension. Instead, your employers pension or personal scheme must provide benefits to match those which SERPS would have provided. You and your employer are both eligible for a rebate on National Insurance contributions – in return for your pension compensating for the SERPS benefits.

There can be times in your life when it is better to be contracted in to SERPS – and times when it is better to be contracted out. As a rule of thumb, it is generally considered better to be contracted out when you are younger because the benefits that you will get from building your own pension will be better than those you might get from SERPS. This is especially true if you are not well paid.

The reason for contracting out should be that the National Insurance contributions rebate for a particular tax year produces a pension larger than the amount of pension which SERPS would have provided. But it is a complicated decision depending on your age and gender. In addition, the changes to the National Insurance contributions rebate system taking effect from April 1997 have altered the previous assumptions about whether or not to contract out for members of certain types of pension scheme. But if you are considering contracting out of SERPS – or switching back in, then discuss the matter with a qualified independent financial adviser.

Graduated Pension Scheme

This is a state pension scheme which existed between 1961 and 1975. If you paid into it you might qualify for a small pension, currently around £6 or £7 a week. Some people were contracted out of it and the contributions were paid into their employers scheme.

Employers pension schemes

ONE OF THE BEST WAYS to start building up your pension income is through an employers pension scheme. A pension can be a very valuable benefit in your employment package mainly because your employer is usually bearing the brunt of the cost of the contributions towards your fund.

Some employers will contribute as much as two-thirds towards your pension, so you would be foolish not to join, even if you don't plan to spend all your working life with that company. There are two main types of company pension scheme.

> Independent financial adviser and *Moneywise* Ask the Professionals panellist Keith Sanham says:
>
> "A pension is a deferred salary. If you can't see why you should join your employer's pension scheme think of your employer's contribution as a pay rise now that is receivable in the future."

FINAL SALARY SCHEMES

Your pension is worked out according to a proportion of your final salary when you retire and the number of years you have worked for the company. The ratio differs from company to company. The most usual ratio is 1/60 of salary, which means that you would get 1/60 of your final salary for every year that you have been a member of the company scheme. If you worked there for 30 years you would get 30/60 or half of your final salary. Ratios can vary between 1/50 and 1/80 of final salary. Normally, you contribute around 5% of your earnings (on which you get tax relief) and your employer makes up the rest. If you belong to a non-contributory pension scheme your employer makes all the contributions.

Advantages

- You know what your pension will be.
- Your pension will rise in line with earnings and inflation of up to 5% a year.
- Some pension schemes will also offer additional discretionary revisions.

Disadvantages

- The proportion on which your final salary is worked out may be poor. If, for example, your scheme offers 1/80 of final salary, this means that you will have to work 40 years to achieve just half your final salary, compared with 25 years if your scheme offered a 1/50 of final salary.
- The final £3,000 or so of your final salary is not counted because it is assumed that this is what the state pension will cover.

Money purchase schemes

These pension schemes are becoming more popular with employers than final salary schemes. You and your employer contribute towards a pension fund but the size of your pension when you retire will depend on how the fund grows and how much you have both contributed. On retirement, you buy an annuity with the fund. An annuity is an insurance contract which pays a regular income. The rate of income you will get will depend on when you buy it as annuity rates fluctuate. There are no guarantees that you will end up with a decent pension.

However, with a money purchase scheme you often have several funds to choose from so you can pick different areas of investment and have more say about where your money is invested.

Advantages

- If you plan to move jobs frequently, money purchase schemes can be a good idea because you can simply move the pot of money you have built up into another scheme.
- You will have some say over how your money is invested.

Disadvantages

- There is no direct link to inflation so you may not be protected against rising prices.
- If you and your employer contribute too little, your pension fund will be small.
- Poor investment performance may inhibit pension growth.
- You may get a poor annuity rate when you draw your pension.

Benefits

The Inland Revenue imposes a limit on the benefits you will get out of your employer's pension. Your pension cannot be more

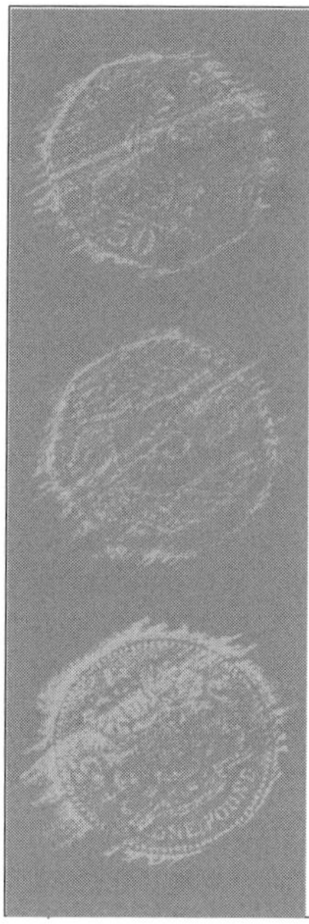

INLAND REVENUE LIMITS ON BENEFITS FROM AN EMPLOYERS PENSION

Type of benefit	Post-1989	1987–89	Pre-1987
Pension at retirement	2/3 final pay pay to max. £56,000	2/3 final pay	2/3 final pay
Tax-free lump sum at retirement	1·5 times final pay to max. £126,000	1·5 times final pay to max. £150,000	1·5 times final pay
Life insurance	4 times final pay to max. £336,000	4 times final pay	4 times final pay
Survivor pension	4/9 final pay to max. £37,333	4/9 final pay	4/9 final pay

than two-thirds of your final salary – whether the scheme you're in is final salary or money purchase. The definition of final salary and other limits depends on when you joined the employers scheme. The other limits apply to the tax-free lump sum to which you may be entitled, life insurance and widow(er)s pension.

- *Post-1989 regime*: These limits apply to you if you belong to a scheme that was set up on or after 14 March 1989, or your scheme was already set up but you joined it on or after 1 June 1989. They can also apply if you elect to be covered by this regime.
- *1987/89 regime*: These limits apply if you belong to a scheme that was set up before 14 March 1989 which you joined on or after 17 March 1987 and before 1 June 1989.
- *Pre-1987 regime*: These limits apply if you joined your scheme before 17 March 1987.

For post-1989 members there is a limit on the the size of the final salary on which you can base your pension. In 1997/98, the earnings cap is set at £84,000. This means that you cannot take any salary over and above £84,000 into account when calculating your pension. Even if you earn £100,000, your maximum final salary is still £84,000 for the purpose of your pension – and the maximum allowable pension is £56,000, two-thirds of that amount.

The important thing to remember about the earnings cap is that it applies only to post-1989 members. So if you fall into one of the other categories described above, the earnings cap does not apply to you. Pre-1987 and 1987–89 members can still take their full final salaries into account when planning their pensions – and should be wary of switching to a new pension as the earnings cap will then apply.

RETIREMENT DATE

Pensions used to be provided for men at 65 and women at 60 but as the state retirement age is due to be reset at 65 for both sexes many company schemes are moving towards this date. Under Inland Revenue rules you must take retirement between 50 and 75 if the Post-1989 regime applies, or between 60 and 75 in most other cases.

If you want to retire before the retirement date set by your pension scheme you will have to take a reduced pension because you will have made fewer contributions and you will not have had enough time for your fund to build up to its full potential. Also, if you retire earlier, you are more likely to live longer and so the pension will have to pay out for longer.

If you have to retire because of ill health, then the rules for a final-salary scheme allow you to retire on the pension you would have received at your normal retirement age, calculated as a proportion of your current salary. The only condition is that there must be 20 years between the date of your joining the scheme and the date when you would normally have retired – otherwise the benefits are reduced.

If you are medically certified as having a very short life expectancy then you can exchange your entire pension entitlement for a cash lump sum. In this circumstance, part of the lump sum will be considered as the equivalent of the one you could have taken in exchange for part of your pension (the equivalent of 1·5 times your pensionable salary). This part of the money will be tax-free. Any further lump sum cash in excess of the tax-free element will be taxed.

If you are in a money purchase scheme and you retire early because of illness, then your position may be very poor, since your pension will again be based on the much smaller fund which you have been able to accumulate prior to your retirement. If your life expectancy is very short, then you may be able to purchase an annuity from a firm specialising in this area – often referred to as 'impaired lives' – which will pay a much more favourable income, because you are not expected to live very long.

In cases where you retire early because of ill health, your company scheme may make discretionary payments, or cover may be available under the company's group income replacement insurance scheme (see Chapter 4 page 86).

Contributions

You are not allowed to contribute more than 15% of your salary to your company scheme. Like final salary, your salary for the purpose of pension contributions is your basic salary plus bonuses, overtime, and other taxable benefits such as company cars. Where the earnings cap applies – to post-1989 members – then you can contribute a maximum of 15% of your salary up to the earnings cap of £84,000 (1997/98).

Example
If you joined your employers pension scheme in the 1997/98 tax year and your salary is £30,000, under the Inland Revenue rules you can contribute up to 15% of £30,000 (£4,500) to an employers pension that year. If your salary is £95,000, you could contribute 15% of £84,000 which is £12,600. You can't contribute 15% of your full salary because it is over the earnings cap.

There is, however, no limit on how much your employer can contribute to your pension. The amount is as much as is necessary to make sure the scheme meets all of its liabilities – this is most important with final salary scheme.

As the earnings cap is high, you might not think that it affects you, but it has not been increased every year. And when it is, the amount is in line with the RPI (Retail Price Index), which moves more slowly than average earnings. Therefore, the real value of the cap is actually decreasing. and you may be caught out if you are still a long way off retirement.

Personal pensions

Personal pensions work in the same way as company money purchase schemes (see page 113) except you are making all the contributions into the fund. When you retire you can take up to 25% of the fund value as a tax-free lump sum and you must use the rest to buy an annuity to provide you with an income for the rest of your life.

Personal pensions can offer a lot of flexibility. You can choose how much money you want to invest, where you want to invest it and how much risk you want to take. These pensions usually work in one of two ways:

- *Unit-linked*: This is the riskier type of pension. You buy units in a fund of shares and choose your level of risk according to the type of fund you choose. It could be in a UK fund or a riskier specialist fund. The value of your pension will depend on how that fund is performing when you retire. If the stockmarket is rising you will do well but if it is doing badly you will not be looking forward to a comfortable retirement. Some unit-linked pensions give you the option to transfer your money to a safer deposit-based fund before you retire so that you don't risk losing everything
- *With-profits*: As with a unit-linked plan, you buy units in a fund of shares but the risk you take is less. Every year you will get a bonus added to your fund which cannot be taken away. The size of this bonus will depend on how well the investment has performed that year. Any minor fluctuations in performance are smoothed out because if the fund does well, some of the profit will be kept back to bolster up the bonuses during the leaner years. But up to half the growth will come from a terminal bonus which is paid out at the end of the pension's term.

Benefits

The big difference between employers pensions and personal pensions is that there is no maximum limit to a personal pension. The pension you take from your personal pension plan depends on how much you contribute, how successfully the fund is managed, your gender and chosen retirement age, and the annuity rate you purchase. It does limit the size of tax-free lump sum you can take.

You can set up your personal pension in a variety of ways. It can be like an employers money purchase pension, where you buy the annuity on retirement, or you can set it up in segments and buy annuities at different stages throughout retirement. It is only worth taking a phased retirement pension if you'll have a fund of £100,000 or more because you will pay higher charges than on a standard plan.

You can also set up your personal pension so you have the option to defer buying your annuity any time up to the age of 75. You can withdraw some of the cash from your fund to tide you over but leave the rest of the fund intact. This is known as drawdown. This can work in your favour on retirement, if at that time you think annuity rates are going to rise in the future. It can also be advantageous if you think you may not live until you are 75, because the fund can be left to your heirs. However, the reverse may also happen and rates may fall.

Retirement age

You can take the pension from a personal pension plan at any time between the ages of 50 and 75. You specify the age when you set up the personal pension, and you do not have to have your employer's permission. You do not have to retire in order to take your pension. You can start to draw your pension, and keep on working at the same time.

People in some occupations can retire at earlier ages which have been agreed with the Inland Revenue: footballers and dancers, for example, can retire at 35, and cricketers and trapeze artists can retire at 40.

Early retirement isn't an option with a personal pension scheme, except for occupations of the type discussed above where the Inland Revenue has agreed special conditions. Instead, when you start your personal pension, you should consider very carefully the age at which you want to retire. Remember that a

Inland Revenue limits on contributions into a personal pension	
Age 35 and under	17.5% of earnings
Age 36 to 45	20% of earnings
Age 46 to 50	25% of earnings
Age 51 to 55	30% of earnings
Age 56 to 60	35% of earnings
Age 61 to 75	40% of earnings

personal pension can mature when you are aged 50 or over – so your early retirement can be built into the plan from the start.

If you are unable to continue your normal occupation, or an occupation for which you trained, as a result of illness or incapacity, you may be able to retire earlier than 50. You will need to have suitable medical evidence of your incapacity. In such circumstances your pension scheme may allow you to take your pension early. In this case the same process applies as would have done if you had retired at the normal age. Your pension fund will be used to purchase an annuity, which will provide a pension income for you. However, the income you receive may be small, and certainly will be much poorer than the pension you might have expected at normal retirement:

- There will have been less time to build up your pension fund through contributions and through the investment gain.
- Your life expectancy may still be quite long, and therefore the annuity will pay a less favourable rate than you could have expected at a later age, because the annuity will have to pay an income to you for much longer.

Contributions

You can pay as much or as little as you can afford into a personal pension but, obviously, the more you pay in the the greater the chance the fund will have of growing. You can pay the same amount each month or pay different amounts. You can even make one contribution a year, which can be useful when you are self-employed and are not exactly sure how much income you will have each month.

Although the money you put into a pension fund attracts tax relief, the Inland Revenue sets a limit on how much you can put into the fund each year, on a sliding scale according to your age. The table on page 119 shows how much you can contribute.

Your earnings for pensions purposes are your 'net relevant earnings' – this is basically your taxable income, or your taxable profits if you're self-employed. You cannot contribute more than a proportion of £84,000, which is the earnings cap for 1997/98. Anything you earn over this limit will not be counted towards your pension.

If you don't make the maximum contributions each year, you can use the Inland Revenue 'carry back' and 'carry forward' rules which allows you to catch up on any unused contributions that you failed to make over the previous six years (see page 126).

If you don't belong to a company scheme, you can take out more than one personal pension as long as you stay within the Inland Revenue maximum contribution limits. However, each personal pension has its own administration charges so don't spread your money too thinly.

Where can you buy a personal pension?

There are many routes to getting a pension but after all the stories in the press about pensions mis-selling it is worth taking your time and the right advice before you sign up for anything.

- An independent financial adviser will be able to go through all the products on the market and come up with those which are suitable for you.
- Your bank, building society or insurance company can give you advice but in most cases the salesperson will only be recommending their own products if they are what as known as 'tied agents'. Some companies offer you a choice but their choices are usually only made from a selected panel of products, not the entire market.
- A direct provider, such as Virgin Direct or Marks & Spencer, will cut out the intermediary and claim to offer you a cheaper product because there is no commission to pay and fewer overheads to account for. But be sure that the pension is one that is suited to your needs and check investment performance. You may save on some initial charges but they could be wiped out by a poor investment performance.

Personal pension checklist

1 Is it flexible?

- ❍ Can you start and stop your contributions when you want to without risking a penalty?
- ❍ Can you reduce your pension contributions without risking a penalty?
- ❍ Can you choose when you pay in contributions (i.e., monthly or annually)?
- ❍ Can you vary the amount that you pay in?
- ❍ If, later, you get the chance to join a company pension scheme can you convert your personal pension into a freestanding additional voluntary contribution plan without risking penalties? This would convert it into a top-up policy that would run alongside your company pension plan.
- ❍ Do you pay lower charges if you pay single premiums? This can be a useful saving if you are self-employed.

2 How much are its charges?

- ❍ How much will you have to pay in initial set-up charges?
- ❍ Is there an annual management charge?
- ❍ Is there a monthly administration charge?
- ❍ Are there any extra charges?
- ❍ Does investment performance make the charges seem reasonable or even negligible?

3 Investment performance

- ❍ How much risk are you prepared to take?
- ❍ Does this pension fund match your level of risk?
- ❍ Has the company got a good consistent track record?
- ❍ If you want to change your investment priorities, for example, take more or less risk, does the company offer enough funds for you to switch?

4 If you can't work

- ❍ Does your pension offer a waiver of premium benefit and pay the contributions on your behalf while you are sick or injured?
- ❍ Does it pay contributions up to retirement age?
- ❍ Does it charge for waiver of premium benefit?
- ❍ Does it offer cover for the self-employed?

There are several factors you need to take into account before you commit yourself to a personal pension, including investment performance, charges, and the flexibility of the pension. Use the checklist to identify the options you want and run the details of any scheme you're considering against the list.

Checking your pension's progress

IT'S IMPORTANT TO KEEP TRACK of how your pension arrangements are developing. It's a good idea to look carefully at any information you receive from pension providers.

STATE PENSIONS

You can get a forecast of your Basic State Pension and your SERPS pension by completing Form BR19 'Request for a Retirement Pension Forecast' from your local Benefits Agency office.

Send it to the DSS, and they will provide you with a forecast based on your working record to date, and assumptions about your work in the future, assuming that you continue working until your state retirement age.

If there are gaps in your National Insurance contributions record, your forecast will be less than the maximum pension. Find out if you're eligible for any credits – if not it could be worth making voluntary contributions (see page 110).

EMPLOYERS SCHEMES

- *Final salary*: You'll receive an annual statement giving the details of the benefits you can expect on retirement. All figures will be given in terms of your current salary, so it gives you an indication of your pension in today's values. Since most people can assume that their salary will increase at least in line with inflation, this is a useful indicator of the standard of living you can expect from your pension. Remember that this is a forecast – if you leave the scheme or retire earlier than the normal scheme retirement date, then the pension you will receive will be less than the projection which is made today.
- *Money purchase schemes*: In a money purchase scheme your final pension depends entirely on the underlying performance of the assets invested on your behalf. There is no guaranteed pension when you retire. You'll get an annual statement which shows the assumed pension you would be able to buy with the projected fund. With these schemes, you're vulnerable to the fluctuations of the investment market. so it is much more important for you to be

aware of the pension fund's performance than if you were in a final salary scheme. If you are in this type of scheme, you can take a more active role in deciding the fund in which your assets are invested, rather than simply leaving it to the pension fund managers. So if you think performance isn't very good you could consider switching – but consult your pension manager first.

Personal pensions

You get an annual statement on your pension's performance. Be aware that the assumptions used are examples only. The actual performance may be different. *Money Management* and *Pensions Management Monthly* publish monthly statistics to help you track performance.

If you are unhappy about the way your pension is performing, you should not rush to do anything for a while. It may be a temporary blip and recovery could be fairly swift. If, however, it seems to be slipping further down the performance tables, with no sign of a turnaround, there are several things you can do.

You might be able to switch the asset allocations within the fund you've got. This is particularly prudent when you're coming up to retirement and should be switching out of equities into more stable investments. You may be able to make one free switch a year, which will cost around 0·5% of the fund's value. If your pension is sinking without trace, you could consider moving out of it altogether but this really should be a last course of action. Transferring funds to another pension altogether can be expensive and it may be better to freeze this fund and start a new one, although this could still attract punitive administrative charges. So before you make any serious decisions, take financial advice.

Topping up your pension

Having checked on your pensions progress and worked through the retirement calculator on pages 107–8, you might decide you want to boost your pension contributions. Here are your options.

Employers pension schemes

You can boost your pension by buying additional voluntary contributions (AVCs). However, you should bear in mind that you cannot go over the limit of 15% of your salary. There are three main ways of setting up AVCs:

Through your employer's scheme: All in-house schemes must also offer an AVC scheme but they take different forms depending on your type of pension.

If you belong to a public sector scheme you can use your AVCs to buy added years of membership to increase the number of years on which your pension will be based. This also means that all your benefits based on the pension formula will also be increased automatically.

Through a money purchase scheme: Here you invest your AVCs with an insurance company or building society. The AVCs build up in an investment fund, which you use to buy extra benefits from the main pension scheme.

Through free-standing additional voluntary contributions (FSAVCs): These are similar to in-house AVCs but you choose where you invest them. They are more flexible because you can build them up and then buy extra benefits from the scheme that you belong to at retirement, which may not be the one you joined when you started working. However, you are likely to pay higher charges than with in-house AVCs.

ADDITIONAL BENEFITS

- If you die before your retirement date your AVCs will be returned to your estate.
- You can add life insurance to an AVC plan and get tax relief on the premiums.
- An AVC plan could provide a source of income if you want to retire early.
- If you've taken a career break, this is a good way to catch up on your missed years of pension contributions.
- You aren't allowed to have more than one FSAVC plan but you can, however, pay into an AVC plan and an FSAVC plan at the same time.

Before you decide to take out an AVC plan you should check whether you are allowed to increase the contributions in your main scheme. If you do this, your employer might also match your extra contributions. Your employer can't contribute to an AVC plan.

AVCs can be an inflexible way to save for retirement. If you think you might need the money before you retire it might be

Example of carry forward calculation

Say you are 38 and had net relevant earnings of £25,000 for the 1997/98 tax year. In addition, you inherited £10,000 which you wish to contribute to your personal pension. You can contribute in the 1997/98 tax year as follows:

Tax Year	Age	Net Relevant Earnings	Contribution Limit %	Maximum Allowable Contribution	Actual Contribution	Unused Allowance
97/98	38	£25,000	20%	£5,000	£5,000	£0

You still have £5,000 from your inheritance which you can contribute to your pension. Under carry forward rules, you can look at the six previous years. In these, you had relatively little spare cash, and could not make the maximum allowed contribution in any of those years.

Tax Year	Age	Net Relevant Earnings	Contribution Limit %	Maximum Allowable Contribution	Actual Contribution	Unused Allowance
97/98	38	£25,000	20%	£5,000	£5,000	£0
91/92	32	£16,000	17.5%	£2,800	£1,500	£1,300
92/93	33	£17,500	17.5%	£3,062.50	£1,800	£1,262.50
93/94	34	£18,000	17.5%	£3,150	£1,500	£1,650
94/95	35	£20,000	17.5%	£3,500	£2,000	£1,500
95/96	36	£20,000	20%	£4,000	£2,200	£1,800
96/97	37	£22,000	20%	£4,400	£2,500	£1,900

You can therefore contribute £5,000 to your pension, using your spare relief as follows:

	Available Allowance	Contribution
91/92	£1,300.00	£1,300.00
92/93	£1,262,50	£1,262.50
93/94	£1,650.00	£1,650.00
94/95	£1,500.00	£787.50
95/96	£1,800.00	–
96/97	£1,900.00	–

Next year, if you again have money to invest over and above your 1998/99 allowance, you still have £712.50 of your 1994/95 allowance to use, as well as £3,700 from your 1995/96 and 1996/97 relief.

better to go for a more flexible plan so that you are able to get at your money.

Personal pensions

As long as you're not contributing the maximum already, you can simply increase your contributions. If you are contributing the maximum now, but weren't in the past, you can take advantage of any unused tax relief from previous years, even if you didn't have a pension then. There are two options. You can either carry back or carry forward (see the example on page 125).

Carry back allows you to treat the contributions as though they were made in the preceding tax year to use up that year's tax relief. You don't have to decide how much you are going to contribute until you know what your tax position is for the year just ended.

Carry forward allows you to use up the tax relief for the past six years but you will need to use up the current year's tax relief first. If you need advice on how to do this, get in touch with an IFA. You might also need advice on whether you should contract back into SERPS.

Taking your pension

You might have hoped that once you reach retirement there'll be no more choices to make. But you need to be aware of what should happen as retirement approaches.

State pensions

The DSS should normally send you a claim form, BR1, about four months before your state retirement age. If you do not receive one, then contact your local Benefits Agency for a form.

You have the choice of taking your pension at state retirement age, or of deferring it for up to five years. If you choose the option of deferring your state pension, then you will earn increases to the pension of about 7·5% for each year you defer. After 6 April 2010, these increases will be at a rate of approximately 10·4% a year. If you wish to defer your state pension, complete form BR432, which you will find by obtaining a copy of leaflet NI92

'Giving up your Retirement Pension to earn extra' from your local Benefits Agency.

Final salary employers pension schemes

If you are a member of a final salary employers pension scheme, then you should expect to receive a statement from your scheme about three months before your retirement date. This will state how much your pension should be. If you don't receive this statement, contact your pension scheme administrator. In situations where you have a preserved pension, make sure that the pension scheme knows how to get in touch with you. If the company has moved, and you do not know how to get in touch with it, contact the Pension Schemes Registry for help. It will send you a form (PR4) to fill in.

When you have received details of your benefits under your company scheme, you will need to supply the administrators with basic information, such as details of the bank account into which you wish your pension to be paid. You'll need to decide whether to take a lump sum (see page 130).

Money purchase employers pension schemes and personal pensions

If you belong to a money purchase scheme or have a personal pension, you will build up a fund. Its size will depend on the investment performance and the amount of contributions you have put into it. When you retire you will have the option to take part of the fund as a tax-free lump sum, and you have to buy an annuity with the rest.

An annuity is basically an insurance contract, that you take out in exchange for the lump sum from your pension, which gives you a defined level of income for the rest of your life or a fixed period, whichever you choose.

Choosing which annuity to buy is one of the most important retirement decisions you will make because annuity rates fluctuate all the time and when you retire they may be higher or lower than average. Research from the Annuity Bureau shows that a man aged 65 who has a fund of £75,000 would get an extra £2,000 a year from the best provider compared to the worst provider.

You don't have to buy the annuity offered by your pension provider, there are many to choose from on the open market.

LIFE EXPECTANCY

This table shows how many more years you can expect to live once you've reached the age of 60 and over.

Age	Male	Female
60	18·2	22·2
65	14·5	18·2
70	11·4	14·5
75	8·7	11·3
80	6·5	8·4

Source: The Government Actuary's Department (1995/96)

However, before you rush out to buy, find out if your pension provider charges you for moving to another annuity provider or if it offers a loyalty bonus. It may be worth sticking with your original provider. *Moneywise* carries a table of the latest best buys each month in our Advice pages. It's worth taking professional advice from an IFA or a pensions consultant before you choose which one to buy.

If you've set up your pension in segments, you'll need to shop around for an annuity at different stages of your retirement. If your pension gives you the option to defer buying your annuity, you will need to get some advice as you near retirement on whether to use this option.

The rate of income you'll get will depend on your age, sex and interest rates generally. If you take early retirement your annuity income will be lower because the younger you are when you take annuity, the longer the insurance company will have to pay you an income. Women usually get a lower income than men because they live longer (see life expectancy above).

Annuity rates are linked to the general rate of interest, which is why they fluctuate all the time. The rates tend to be high when the stockmarket is performing badly, and low when it is performing well. Over the last ten years the value of a £10,000 annuity has been as low as £800 and as high as £1,350.

Annuity checklist

Do I need the income now or later?

If you need an income straightaway you can opt for an immediate annuity which will pay you an income from the first day of your retirement. If you can wait for a while, a deferred annuity will pay you a lump sum now and a regular income at an agreed date in the future.

Do I need the same amount of money for each year of my retirement?

If you go for a level annuity the amount of income you receive each year stays the same but will be gradually eroded by inflation. If you want to beat inflation you could choose an escalating annuity which pays a fixed percentage increase, say 5% each year. Or you could choose an index-linked annuity which is linked to the Retail Price Index.

If you go for an increasing annuity, your income in the early years will be lower than a level annuity but it will gradually rise and overtake the level annuity income.

Do I want a high income?

You can buy annuities that will give you a high income but you will have to take a risk that the income will fluctuate. Unit-linked and with-profits annuities are both linked to stockmarket investments.

The income from a unit-linked annuity is linked to the value of the fund so it will go up and down. Also the initial income you receive is likely to be half as much as you would get with a level annuity. A with-profits annuity will pay out a fairly low income to start with but it is boosted by annual bonuses. The bonuses will vary from year to year because they depend on the annuity company's investment performance. See Chapters 8 and 9 for more on unit-linked and with-profits investments.

What will my partner, spouse or child do if I die before them?

A guaranteed annuity will protect some of your money if you die soon after taking out the annuity so your dependants will get back some of your retirement fund. If you have a partner, you can take out a joint life annuity which will continue until the second partner dies. This will pay out a lower income than a single life annuity, which you should take out if you have no dependants and which will stop when you die.

Why does my health matter?

If you are in good health you are likely to live longer and need an income for longer. If you are in poor health you could choose an impaired-life annuity which will pay you a higher income to reflect the fact that you may not live as long. This could be as much as 10% to 15% higher depending on how long the provider thinks you will live, given your medical condition.

You could get an impaired-life annuity if you have suffered from any of the following: cancer, heart disease, stroke, kidney failure or multiple sclerosis. There are also lifestyle annuities for people who smoke, are overweight or diabetic.

Increased life expectancy has also had an effect on pensions because more people are living into their eighties and nineties. Although in the UK the current lifespan of a man is 74 years and a woman 79 years, if a man reaches age 65 he can expect to live for another 14·5 years while a woman can expect to live for another 18·2 years. If a man reaches 75 he can expect to live for another 8·7 years while a woman may live for another 11·3 years. Annuity rates have therefore decreased to reflect that fact that providers are paying out for longer.

As there are many different annuity providers, so there are many different types of annuity. The best one for you will depend on a number of factors, such as how old you are when you buy it, how good your health is and whether you have other sources of income apart from your pension. To decide which one is best for you, use the annuity checklist on page 129.

Payments are usually made each month but if it suits you better, you can receive the payments less frequently. How often you choose to be paid will depend on what other sources of income you have. Some people opt to be paid once a year and put the money into a high-interest cheque account which they then draw income out of. If you have other income to rely on you can invest your annuity income somewhere else and then use it when you need it. If you don't need the income straightaway, some personal pensions allow you to defer it until a time when it will be more useful to you.

Taking a lump sum

If your scheme allows you to take a lump sum, you need to consider whether or not to take it. It's important to remember that taking a lump sum will reduce the size of the pension you can take – so you have to be sure that the reduced pension will be enough for you to live on.

The calculation for working out the reduced pension amount after you take a lump sum is complicated, and will be performed by your pension scheme administrators. As a rough guide, if you are a man of 65, then for each £9 you take as a lump sum, your pension is likely to reduce by £1 a year. For a woman of 60, the pension reduces by £1 a year for each £11 she takes in a lump sum.

Other types of pension

THERE ARE ONE OR TWO other types of pension which may be relevant to you – particularly if you are a high earner.

INVESTMENT TRUST PENSIONS

Instead of investing your money in insurance company funds you invest it in investment trusts. These are public companies, quoted on the Stock Exchange, which invest in the shares of other companies. When you buy shares in an investment trust you are spreading your risk so that if one sector of shares does badly you won't lose out overall. Investment trust pensions have so far performed well because of the long-term growth potential of equity investments. Charges can be lower because you can buy them directly from an investment management firm. You want to make sure that you can switch your money into safer investments as you near retirement.

SELF-INVESTED PERSONAL PENSIONS (SIPPs)

SIPPs allow you to make your own investment choices. Instead of investing in insurance company funds you choose where your money goes. It could be into stocks and shares, property and gilts, or unit trusts and investment trusts as well as insurance company funds. You buy the pension administration from one company and the investment advice from another. Usually your investment manager makes the choices for you and builds up your portfolio. Charges for the administration and the advice are separated so it is easier to see where you money is going, but because they charge a flat fee it is only worth taking out the pension if you can afford to put in at least £10,000 a year or a lump sum of £30,000 to £40,000.

> Independent financial adviser and *Moneywise* Ask The Professionals panellist Kean Seager says:
>
> "The wide investment powers of a SIPP and the capacity for investors to manage their own investments can be real advantages. However, the investors must know what they're doing. Poor investment decisions can prove very costly to the fund."

SIPPs are suitable for experienced investors who have a fair amount of money to invest. Beware of hybrid SIPPs which are run by insurance companies. You must invest a large lump sum in the company before you have access to the investment options.

Funded and unfunded unapproved retirement benefit scheme (FURBs and UURBs)

If you earn more than the upper earnings limit (currently £84,000) or you are already contributing the maximum allowed (see pages 116 and 119 for limits) into an Inland Revenue-approved pension scheme your employer can set up a FURB or an UURB to top up your pension benefits. You don't get the same tax advantages as with normal pension plans because the schemes are unapproved. Therefore, you get no tax relief on contributions and the investment growth is not tax free, but they are more tax-efficient than other forms of saving. With a FURB you can make contributions when you want, there are very few investment restrictions and you can take the whole fund as a lump sum when you retire. With an UURB the benefits are provided without a specific fund being set up.

Executive pensions

Executive pensions are simply personal pensions that are run for senior executives and company directors. With these pensions, you can usually make higher contributions – a good idea if you are a high flyer who needs some extra pension provision, particularly in the years up to retirement.

Small Self-Administered Schemes (SSAS)

These are employers schemes with no more than 12 members. Usually, they will only be directors, since there are considerable risks associated with the scheme. A scheme like this is allowed a range of investment options which would be illegal for an ordinary employers pension:

- They can make loans from the pension fund for the purpose of the company's business.
- They can invest in commercial property which can be used for the company's business.
- The trustees can borrow money to purchase an asset, such as commercial property, if the cost is more than the assets in the fund.
- Schemes can invest in shares of unlisted companies, i.e.

companies which do not have 'full' stockmarket listings and which have not undertaken the rigorous process to achieve that listing.

Last-minute retirement planning

If you are reading this and it is too late, or you are unable to pay into an employers or your own personal pension plan, there are other options open to you to help you boost your income in retirement. Unfortunately, although they will provide an income, it may not be as good as the one you could have had if you had taken out a pension.

Savings and investments

You can generate retirement income through a series of savings and investments. These can be through unit or investment trusts wrapped in a personal equity plan (PEP) to make them more tax-efficient, through direct shareholdings, through tax-exempt special savings (TESSAs), or through building society accounts or National Savings.

Advantages

- With many savings and investments, you can stop and start them when you like, and you can get at the income before you retire. Even if you already have a personal pension, you should boost its value with some well-planned savings and investments.

Disadvantages

- If you want to take advantage of the tax-free status of some investments you will be limited as to how much you can contribute each year. For example, you are only allowed to contribute £6,000 a year into a PEP, while shares may attract capital gains tax when you sell. Savings in a building society, may be eroded by the effects of inflation and be worth less over time.

Use your home

If you own your home, you can either sell it and move to a smaller house or you can release capital through a home income plan. Mortgage-based plans work on the premise that you take out an interest-only mortgage on the value of your home, generally up to a maximum of 75%. You then use the money to buy an annuity to give you an income for life (see page 127 for more details).

Advantages

- If you haven't done any serious retirement planning a safe home income plan can boost your retirement income.

Disadvantages

- If your house forms a large part of your estate you will have less to leave to your heirs.

If you are self-employed

You could sell your business and use what you make from it to fund your retirement but this could be risky.

Advantages

- If your business becomes successful and the overall economy is booming you could make a lot of money. You can also carry on working beyond the official retirement date.

Disadvantages

- At today's rates you will need a retirement fund of at least £100,000 to see you through. Is your business worth that much? And if you sell when the market is down, or you sell because of ill health, you might get a much lower price for the business.

Divorce

Currently, one in three marriages ends in divorce. Because women are more likely to have had an interrupted career – raising a family, for example – and because they are still more likely to be in lower-paid jobs than men, there is a huge disparity between the pension benefits being accumulated by men and women.

Men are likely to have the better pension rights, and therefore, until recently, divorced wives were likely to have very little entitlement to income in retirement. The courts could make an order compensating the woman for the pension benefits she had lost, though this was only an obligation in Scotland. In England and Wales it was not automatic, and depended on the wife making a claim to the court.

The 1995 Pensions Act means that now a court can make an order on the husband's pension scheme, which must pay the wife part of her ex-husband's pension when he retires. This is not the solution the pensions industry would have preferred. They would have liked a clean-break settlement at divorce. Instead, the wife has to wait until the husband retires to have access to the pension benefit. For example, it is not entirely clear what will happen if the husband dies before the wife.

Action plan

- ❍ Work out roughly how much income you'll want in retirement – work through the retirement calculator on page 107.
- ❍ If you don't have any pension arrangements, look into joining your employer's scheme if you can, or a personal pension if you're self-employed.
- ❍ Check that your state pension is on target – if not, consider making voluntary National Insurance contributions.
- ❍ Review your pensions progress on a regular basis – think about making additional voluntary contributions if you're in an employers scheme.
- ❍ If you're in a personal pension and you haven't always made contributions while you've been working, investigate making extra contributions under the carry back and carry forward rules.
- ❍ If retirement is not far away and you're in a money purchase employers scheme or a personal pension, start thinking about the type of annuity you want to buy with your pension fund.
- ❍ If you're about to retire, work out how much of the fund you want to take as a tax-free lump sum within the limits.
- ❍ If you haven't built up a pension and retirement is only a few years away, look into using savings and investments or your home as ways of generating income.

8 Introducing savings and investments

Planning your savings and investments is important because this is where your money can really work for you and where you can make a real difference to your finances. In this chapter we look at the basic principles behind choosing how to save and invest, as well as looking at some different options.

Chapter 9 provides a directory of different types of savings accounts and investments, and Chapter 10 looks at putting all this into practice.

First, you need to have looked through the previous chapters to ensure that you've got the financial priorities sorted out:

- You need to make sure you have the right mortgage and that your payments are in line to clear your debt. See Chapter 5 for getting the best deal on your mortgage.
- You need to be contributing to a pension scheme if you can, either your own or your employer's. See Chapter 7 for more advice on pensions.
- You need to make sure that you and your family are financially protected and that you have the right insurance for your needs. See Chapter 6 for more advice on protecting both yourself and your family.

You also need to make sure that you have enough money set aside in an instant access account to cover everyday expenses and bills. A rule of thumb is to make sure that this account contains sufficient funds to cover you for three months' worth of bills, mortgage payments, insurance payments and everyday expenses, such as food and clothes. Then, if anything goes wrong, you will at least have enough readily available cash to give you time to get back on your feet.

Your savings and investment aims

BEFORE YOU EMBARK ON a savings strategy you need to assess exactly what you are saving for. You will be saving for different things at different times of your life and even at different times of the year. For example, you might be saving for both next year's holiday and your child's university education.

But it will do no good to have your holiday savings locked into a five-year investment or the savings for your child's education in a low-interest bearing account which will be gradually eroded by inflation. You need to find the correct savings option for each type of savings.

Independent financial adviser and *Moneywise* Ask The Professionals panellist Rebekah Kearey says:

"A savings strategy should be created for each new situation you are planning. Follow the strategy through and regularly review it because circumstances and economic situations really do change."

Risk

WHERE YOU PUT YOUR MONEY also depends on your attitude to risk. If you are willing to take a lot of risk you could see a considerable return on your money. If, on the other hand, you are unwilling to take much risk you could see your savings eroded by the rise in inflation.

It's best to adopt a suitable savings strategy and to spread your money across a number of savings and investments so that you can expose your money to some degree of risk but still be sure that you won't lose everything if an investment doesn't do as well as you'd hoped.

There are three broad groups of investment: cash-based, fixed- interest and stockmarket-linked. These three can also be seen as

Savings and investments aim checklist

This checklist identifies some of the savings and investment options which could be suitable for a variety of purposes.

Do I need to save for my long-term future, for example , retirement?
Look at medium- to long-term investments, such as PEPs, TESSAs, endowment policies, National Savings, unit trusts and investment trusts.

Do I need to save for an event over the next five to ten years, for example, a child's education or wedding, or a deposit on a house?
Look at medium-term investments, such as TESSAs, PEPs or National Savings, unit trusts and investment trusts.

Do I need to save for an event over the next year, for example, a new kitchen or a holiday abroad?
Consider saving in a high-interest deposit account, but remember to check the notice period.

Do I need an income from my investments or am I investing for growth?
Some equity-based investments allow you to switch emphasis at different times in your life. Make sure you pick an investment which allows you to do this. Other investments, such as some bonds, will automatically pay you an income.

Do I pay tax and if so, at what rate?
If you're a taxpayer make sure you take advantage of tax-efficient savings, such as PEPs or TESSAs. Once you've exhausted your allowances, you can look at other savings, particularly ones which can help if you're a higher-rate taxpayer. If you're a non-taxpayer, make sure you can claim the tax back easily.

Do I mind paying charges?
Some investments, particularly equity-based ones, impose charges. Find out whether these are likely to be cancelled out or reduced by the performance of the investment.

Can I get at my savings in an emergency?
It's no good having all your money tied up where you can't get at it. You must find out how accessible your savings are.

Will I be charged a penalty for cashing in my investment early?
You need to work out whether you are able to stop or start your savings when you want to or whether you will be charged a penalty for doing so. If you have to pay a penalty, it might not be worth investing in that particular product.

What will happen to interest rates and inflation?
Do you think interest rates are going to fall or rise? Low fixed interest rates that lock you in for a number of years can erode the value of your savings.

low, medium and potentially high risk, and offering low, medium and potentially high returns respectively. The returns on equities have far outweighed the returns on building society deposits, even allowing for fluctuations in the stockmarket. It is worth working out how much you can afford to put into equity-based investments and, remember, you don't have to take any more risk than you are comfortable with.

By combining savings and investments in suitable proportions your savings and investments will be balanced. Our savings and investments directory on pages 149–83 is arranged according to the levels of risk. The same degree of risk won't be suitable for everyone and it shouldn't remain the same at all times. The right proportions vary according to your circumstances, your attitude to risk and economic conditions.

Note that this is a rough guide. Any investment can be risky if it is not appropriate for you. The personal circumstances which influence your choice of investments include how much money you've got to invest, the length of time you're able or willing to tie it up for and your age. If, for example, you're nearing retirement it makes sense to realise any gains you've made in stockmarket-linked investments and shift the balance back to a position where the emphasis is on lower-risk investments.

If you've sorted out your financial strategy and you are sure that your finances and your family are protected, you should consider putting some of your money into high-risk investments.

Independent financial adviser and *Moneywise* Ask The Professionals panellist Rebekah Kearey says:

"High-risk investment should only be considered after a secure base has been created using deposits and built up using lower-risk products. They are most usually appropriate for longer-term investors using money that need not be realised at a specific time in the future and importantly by people who acknowledge they may lose it all. Only that part of a portfolio which isn't earmarked for specific purposes should be used."

Independent financial adviser and *Moneywise* Ask The Professionals panellist Rebekah Kearey says:

"Each investment added to your portfolio should fit a specific need. A 2% discount on a guaranteed income bond does not make it appropriate for a growth portfolio.
Similarly, although a high-risk investment in a Latin American unit trust could produce exceptional growth, it is only appropriate if you are not risk averse."

Savings and investments risk checklist

KEY:
*** VERY LOW RISK ****** VERY HIGH RISK**

*
Deposit accounts
TESSAs
National Savings
Guaranteed income bonds

**
Corporate bond PEPs
With-profits bonds
Direct investments in gilts

***
Managed investment bonds
Low-risk UK unit trusts and investment trusts, such as blue chip funds and tracker funds
Guaranteed equity bonds

****
International unit trusts and investment trusts spread across sectors

*****
Single company PEPs
Direct shareholdings in blue chip companies
UK smaller companies unit trusts and investment trusts
Regional unit trusts and investment trusts, such as Europe or North America

******
Direct shareholdings in smaller companies
High-risk unit trusts and investment trusts, such as emerging markets, venture capital or single sectors

We have not included extremely speculative investments.

TIPS FOR HIGH-RISK INVESTING

If you don't want to lose too much of your money follow these tips:

- Only look at regulated investments.
- Don't invest more money than you can afford to lose.
- Don't invest more than 5% of your portfolio.
- Look at collective investments, such as unit trusts or investment trusts.
- Look at the fund manager's performance.
- Only opt for medium- to long-term investments (five to ten years minimum).
- Don't bail out straightaway if your investment falls. It will fluctuate much more more than less risky investments.

Tax

AS EXPLAINED IN CHAPTER 3, there are two taxes which can affect your savings and investments. You have to pay income tax on any interest or dividends, and you may have to pay capital gains tax when you sell (see chapter 3).

YOUR FINANCES

There are some tax breaks though. TESSAs are savings accounts offered by banks and building societies which provide a tax-free return as long as you tie up the money for five years. For more details on TESSAs, see page 150. You can also hold certain shares, unit trusts and investment trusts and corporate bonds in a Personal Equity Plan (PEP) to get a tax-free return. PEPs were set up by the government in 1987 as a way of persuading ordinary investors to invest in the stockmarket. This is how they work:

- You must be over 18 and a UK resident to take out a PEP. You can't jointly own one but a husband and wife can each have a PEP.
- You can put up to £6,000 each year in a general PEP and up to £3,000 a year in a single company PEP. You can either put this money into your PEP as a lump sum or through a monthly savings plan.
- You are allowed to take out only one general and one single PEP each year. This means that you can't divide your £6,000 or £3,000 among different funds.
- You have to invest through an authorised plan manager. This could be a fund manager, stockbroker or an investment adviser – but with some PEPs you can manage the investments, in other words, you decide which shares or trusts to buy and sell – and when.
- All the returns on your PEP are free of both income tax and capital gains tax. You don't even have to declare that you have a PEP on your tax return.
- You can't carry back PEP allowances. So once the tax year has ended you lose any unused PEP allowances.
- The PEP investments you are allowed to invest in are: shares, unit trusts, investment trusts which are quoted on, or invest in, European Union (EU) markets only. To qualify for PEP status, the funds must invest at least 50% of their assets in the EU.

Some types of corporate bonds also qualify (see page 158).

- You are also allowed to invest £1,500 of your general PEP allowance each year in a non-qualifying investment. That means funds which do not fulfil the 50% EU rule.

You will pay charges on PEPs. Initial charges can vary from 0% to 6% of the fund value. You'll also have to pay an annual management charge of around 1%. If you're investing in an investment trust you may have to pay dealing charges. You may also be penalised for early withdrawals or early encashment of your investment.

You can keep your PEP for as long as you like and you can take money out of it at any time. Once you have taken the money out, though, it ceases to have tax-free status. If you are not happy with your PEP's performance you can switch to another fund which is better performing.

Some PEPs offer the guarantee that whatever happens to the stockmarket, you will get back your original investment in full; others offer you the guarantee that your original investment can only fall by a small amount over set periods, so that you know that you are not going to lose the bulk of your investment. These PEPs are suitable for people who are very risk averse, but they can never offer the returns of PEPs that invest all your capital in a rising stockmarket.

Offshore investments

Offshore accounts used to have a slightly dodgy image to them, conjuring up money-laundering antics of drug barons and bank robbers. But investing in an offshore savings account or investment fund is a perfectly legitimate way to reduce or defer your tax bill and is particularly useful if you've already used up your tax allowances in PEPs and TESSAs but still have money to save or invest.

Many offshore accounts are held in British waters, the Isle of Man or the Channel Islands, for example, while other leading offshore centres are firmly on dry land, in Dublin and Luxembourg. There are number of ways to invest in offshore accounts depending on the level of risk you want to take.

Current accounts

Some high street banks and building societies, such as the Woolwich, Northern Rock, Portman and Birmingham Midshires operate offshore instant access or notice accounts, offering interest rates much above their normal high street rates. In xx 1997, a Northern Rock Offshore instant account was paying 6.2% gross on a minimum balance of £10,000 while its high street equivalent was paying 1.5% gross. These are suitable for low-risk investors.

Investment funds

Many of the UK's leading investment companies, such as Schroders and Gartmore, operate offshore investment funds, where you can invest in international equities, bonds and riskier investments such as derivatives. Offshore funds are either open-ended like unit trusts or closed-ended like investment trusts. Open-ended investment companies, which operate like hybrid unit trusts and investment trusts (see page 169) also have a strong presence offshore because they are popular with European investors who don't understand the concepts of unit trusts and investment trusts.

Offshore funds usually perform just as well as their onshore equivalents, often simply because they are managed by the same fund managers. However, with offshore investment funds you usually have to pay a performance fee, which arguably gives the fund manager a big incentive to do his or her best to give a good performance.

Multi-currency cheque accounts

If you own property abroad or are planning to work abroad or have family who live abroad, it can be useful to open a multi-currency cheque account. As the name suggests you are provided with a cheque book which allows you to write cheques in a variety of currencies from French francs, to German deutschmarks to Spanish pesetas. You can even write cheques in American dollars, Japanese yen and ECUs. Multi-currency cheque accounts work in the same way as normal bank accounts; you can withdraw money when you want and set up direct debits and standing orders. Many banks will stipulate that you keep a minimum balance of around £2,500, but you can use multi-currency accounts to cash in on the best rates of exchange around the world.

Money funds

You can also invest in money funds, which pool investors' cash to qualify for wholesale exchange rates on the international money markets. Each currency is represented by its own class of share and the price will vary according to the underlying interest rates. Your shares, which are not in your own base currency, are exposed to the ups and downs of international exchange rates. Although the rewards can be high, these investments are not for the nervous investor.

Tax planning

The main advantages of holding an offshore account for most investors are in terms of tax planning. There are three main advantages:

- If you hold an offshore building society account, you will automatically be paid interest without any tax being deducted from your offshore account. In the UK your savings in a building society account will only be tax free if you are a non-taxpayer, but you will have to claim the tax back yourself.
- You can use offshore accounts or investments to defer the tax you have to pay on savings by having the gross interest capitalised on your account as at 1 May. This then becomes the date at which your account is taxed. However, you don't have to declare the gross interest on your account until the following April, 11 months later, so you can benefit from the tax deferral period. This can be particularly useful if you have used up your £9,000 PEP allowance.
- Because you only pay tax in the band to which you belong when your bill is due, you can defer your tax bill until you retire or become a lower-rate taxpayer. You can put your money into an offshore roll-up fund, for example, which focuses on UK and international equities and bonds, as well as riskier investments, such as derivatives. These funds don't pay out annual dividends, which are taxable, so the growth is rolled up until you decide to cash in your investment. Many offshore funds operate umbrella funds, so you can switch your money around if your investment needs change.

Ethical investments

BEFORE WE ALL STARTED RECYCLING our bottles and driving cars that run on unleaded fuel, anything that was labelled green appeared to be well-meaning but ineffectual. The same cannot be said of ethical investments. Fairly new to the investment market (most are less than ten years old) ethical unit and investment trusts have been some of the best performers on the market.

About £1bn is now invested in 30 UK unit and investment trusts. In addition to ethical investments, there are ethical banks and building society accounts and ethical share portfolio management services. You can even get ethical mortgages, pensions and health insurance.

The main aim of ethical investments is twofold. They aim to invest in companies whose products:

- Do not damage the environment, people or animals.
- Make the environment or community a better place to live.

Ethical unit and investment trusts operate in exactly the same way as conventional trusts in that they buy baskets of shares in a chosen sector (see page 163 for more details on how they work), but before they make the decision to invest in a company, an ethical fund manager will run checks on that company to find out if it has interests in a number of areas according to pre-determined criteria. These might include tobacco, alcohol, armaments, oppressive regimes, use of child labour, vivisection and pornography. Once these checks have been completed, the company will be checked for its positive qualities: Does it have a good track record in the community? Does it have good relations with staff and customers? for example.

Investors can also raise concerns, and affect what the fund invests in. Some of the most recent concerns have been voiced over the level of directors' pay and companies which invest in road-building programmes. An ethical fund will list all the areas which it has screened. If the area in which you have concerns is not listed, this could mean that the fund has invested in it. So you will need to check with the fund manager.

If you are interested in ethical investments, ask an independent financial adviser to recommend some products, or look in the Advice pages of *Moneywise* each month to find out which are the best performing ethical trusts. Before you invest in an ethical product, decide what concerns you, and then try to find a product that will match your investment and ethical needs. There are several ethical investment managers who specialise in giving the right advice to would-be investors. Some of these companies will offer a portfolio screening service, so if you already own shares but have no idea what the companies have interests in, the service will screen the shares to establish their ethical validity. It can also recommend a suitable portfolio if you are interested in buying shares.

If you are interested in ethical banks and building societies, there are a few which ethically screen their business. These include the Co-operative Bank, Shared Interest and Triodos Bank. If you want to take out an ethical mortgage, contact the Ecology Building Society which offers mortgages and savings accounts.

Ethical investments are suitable for most people – if you choose to invest ethically you need not compromise your investment returns. For more information, contact the Ethical Investment Research Service (EIRS) on 0171 735 1351.

Action plan

Before you sign on the dotted line for any savings or investment option, work through the following checklist.

- ❍ Does this investment really cater for my financial needs?
- ❍ Is there a risk that the value of my capital can go down, as well as up?
- ❍ Does the investment pay an income, and is that fixed or variable?
- ❍ What is the best possible return I could get on my money?
- ❍ What is the worst possible return I could get on my money?
- ❍ What will happen to the investment if I die?
- ❍ Can I get out of my investment easily or change my level of contributions, or will I have to pay penalties?
- ❍ How risky is my investment? Look at the risk to capital, the risk that interest rates will fluctuate, inflation will rise, the investment provider will go bust.
- ❍ How do the returns on my investment compare to similar products?
- ❍ Will my investment be taxed?

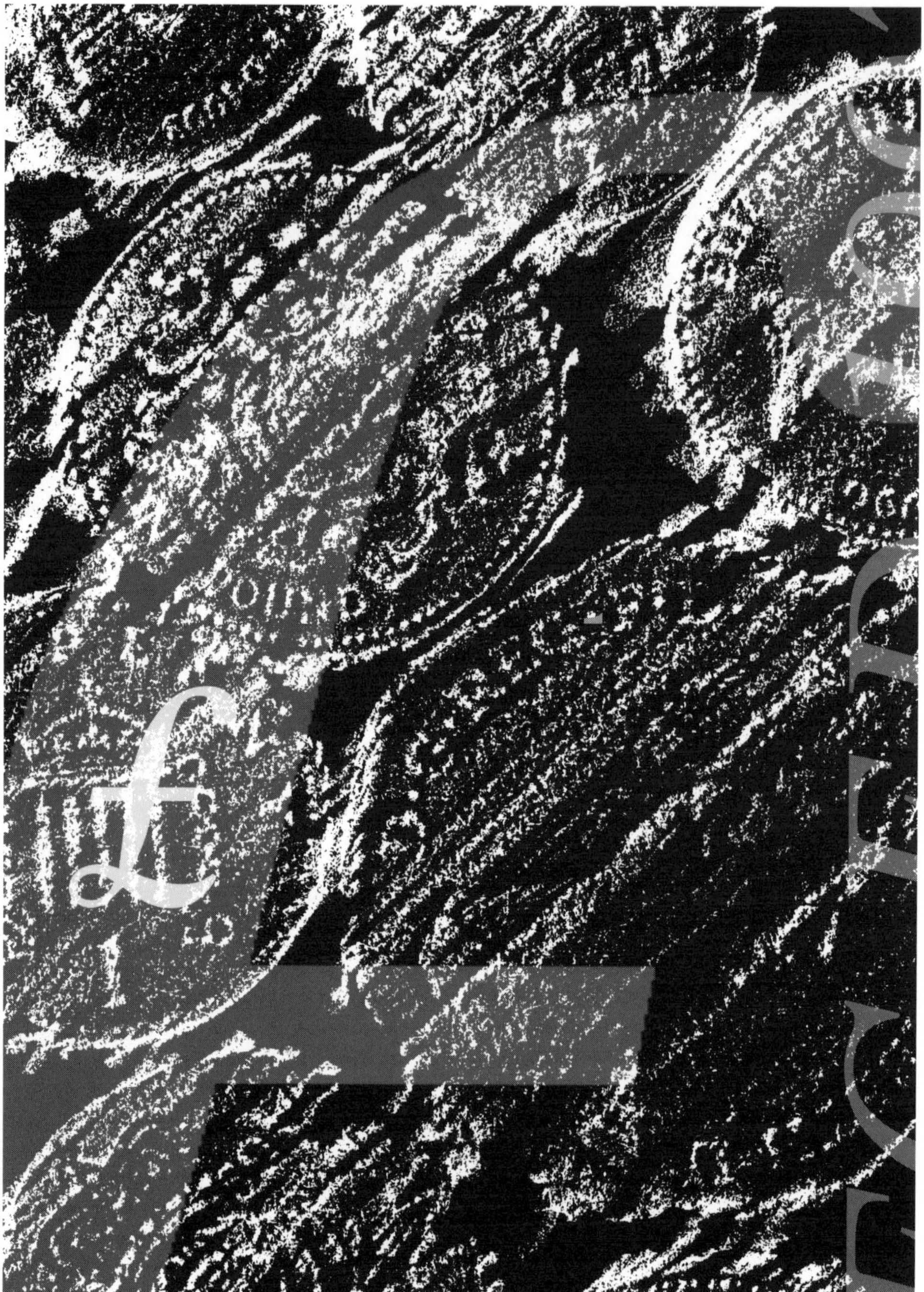

9
Directory of savings and investments

This chapter is a directory of different types of saving and investment options: Low-risk investments starting on this page, low- to medium-risk starting on page 156, medium- to high-risk starting on page 163 and high-risk investments starting on page 175.

Low-risk investments

THIS GROUP INCLUDES the basic and probably more familiar homes for your savings: bank and building society accounts. There is a range of different types of account – does the one you've got really meet your requirements? This section also includes the National Savings products.

Banks and building society accounts

INSTANT ACCESS ACCOUNTS

You can normally open an instant access account with a minimum investment of £1, but some higher interest paying accounts may require more. Interest is either paid annually or twice yearly and is calculated daily. You do not pay any charges for holding an instant access account.

Suitable for: People who want to get at their money quickly; interest rates are usually higher than those paid on a current account.

NOTICE ACCOUNTS

The minimum investment usually needed to open a notice account is around £500 and, as the name suggests, you can't get at your money straightaway. You will have to wait a minimum of 30 days and even up to 180 days, depending on the terms of your account. Your reward for waiting is that you get a higher rate of interest paid on your account. Interest rates are variable and are paid according to the terms of the account. You have to follow the terms of the account to avoid paying penalties. So if you have a 180-day notice account and you need to draw out the money before the notice period is up you will have to pay a penalty.

Suitable for: People who want a safe home for their money, don't need to dip constantly into their savings account and want a higher rate of interest than on offer with an instant access account.

Fixed-rate bonds

Banks and building societies also offer accounts or bonds at a fixed rate for between one and five years. At the end of the term the account is closed and you can draw out the money without giving notice. With fixed-rate bonds there is a risk that you will lose out if interest rates rise after you have deposited your money. If you want to withdraw your cash before the fixed-rate term is up you face having to pay severe penalties.

Suitable for: People who want a higher rate of interest but don't need to dip into their savings accounts at regular intervals.

Tax-exempt special savings accounts (TESSAs)

If you want the potential to earn interest which is free of tax you can choose to save in a TESSA. If you are over 18 you can invest up to £9,000 over five years in this type of account. The rules allow you to deposit up to £3,000 in the first year and then up to £1,800 a year in the next four years.

All the interest you earn on a TESSA is tax free if you leave it there for five years, but if you have to withdraw any of the money, your TESSA may be closed and you will be taxed on the interest as if it was all earned in the year in which you closed the account. Some TESSAs do allow you to make withdrawals but you can only withdraw the interest, which will be taxed at 20%.

Interest may be either fixed or variable, and you won't pay any charges, but there may be penalties if you dip into the account early or transfer your money to another TESSA. You should therefore find out what the penalties are before you open the account. Terms can vary from as little as two weeks' notice to 180 days' notice and 180 days' loss of interest.

Suitable for: People who want a higher rate of interest than a bank or building society account and the chance to earn interest free of tax. In July 1997, the top-rate TESSAs were paying 7·6%. A TESSA can be worth considering even if you don't intend to hold the money in it for five years because taking interest net of tax rates can be more competitive than instant access accounts.

Follow-on TESSAs

When your TESSA matures, unless you transfer it into a follow-on TESSA your money will be transferred into an ordinary savings account. You can then decide what you want to do with the money next.

If you invested the full £9,000 in your first TESSA you can reinvest the £9,000 into a follow-on TESSA within six months of it maturing but you can't reinvest any of the interest you earned. Once you've reinvested the £9,000 you can't pay in any more in subsequent years. If you don't reinvest the full £9,000 you can invest up to £1,800 each year over the next four years as long as you don't exceed the £9,000 limit. If you invested less than £3,000 over five years in your first TESSA, you can reinvest the interest as well as the capital.

Building society windfalls

If you are one of the 20 million building society qualifying account-holders who was paid a windfall bonus from one of the demutualising building societies, you might be hoping to strike lucky again.

Investment experts think that yet more building societies will demutualise over the next few years and many of the smaller building societies will merge or become takeover targets as they find it more difficult to compete in a streamlined market.

It is impossible to say which building society will be next. As this book was published, some of the larger ones, such as Nationwide and Bradford & Bingley, said they were firmly committed to mutual status and had increased minimum qualifying investments to discourage carpetbaggers (people who open accounts with a minimum balance simply to take advantage of the fact that the building society may demutualise).

Opening accounts in several building societies in the hope that they will demutualise is all right if you have the money to do it, but you should not put all your savings into these accounts in the hope that they will eventually pay out. It is far better to look at other savings and investments that will give you a higher return for your money. You can also look at other building society investments such as TESSAs (see page 150) or PIBs (see page 170), which may pay out a windfall bonus should the building society decide to demutualise.

If you do open a building society account, check that it is an account which gives you membership status – not all do and there have been some very disappointed investors. Also, make sure that you don't let your balance dip below the qualifying minimum. Otherwise you could lose out.

National Savings

ANOTHER WAY TO MAKE tax-efficient savings is to put your money into National Savings, the government-run savings scheme. This can be a particularly safe home for your money and rates on some accounts are competitive.

Some of theses accounts offer tax-free benefits, while others are specifically aimed at children or pensioners. You can open National Savings accounts at post offices or direct from the National Savings (Helpline: 0645 645000).

NATIONAL SAVINGS ORDINARY ACCOUNT

Minimum deposit: £10
Maximum deposit: £10,000
Charges: None
Withdrawal notice: None
Interest rates: From 1·5%
Special features: The first £70 of interest you earn is tax free; children and adults can open an account.
Drawbacks: Interest rates are currently not very competitive. You can only draw out £100 in one go unless you apply for a Regular Customer Account, which will allow you to draw out £250 in one go.
Suitable for: Savers with small amounts who also need instant access.

National Savings Investment Account

Minimum deposit: £20
Maximum deposit: £100,000
Charges: None
Withdrawal notice: One month
Interest rates: From 4·75%
Special features: Competitive interest rates with banks and building societies. Good if you are a non-taxpayer because interest is paid gross so there is no need to reclaim the tax.
Drawbacks: None worth mentioning
Suitable for: Savers with small amounts who do not need instant access.

National Savings Capital Bonds

Minimum purchase: £100
Maximum purchase: £250,000
Charges: None
Early cash-in penalties: None
Interest rates: Fixed for five years. Series J 6·65% a year. The rate you get increases each year.
Special features: Bonds are intended as a five-year investment and interest is payable at the end of the five-year term or when you cash in the bond. Good for non-taxpayers because the interest credited is gross.
Drawbacks: If you are a taxpayer you must pay tax on the interest.
Suitable for: Non-taxpayers who aren't eligible for either Children's Bonus Bonds or Pensioners Bonds (see pages 155–6).

National Savings Income Bonds

Minimum purchase: £2,000 (bought in multiples of £1,000).
Maximum purchase: £250,000
Charges: None
Withdrawal notice: Three months. Money can only be withdrawn in multiples of £1,000.
Early cash-in penalties: You earn interest at half the usual rate if you cash the bonds within the first year.
Interest rates: Variable and currently paying 6·5%.
Special features: These type of bonds pay very competitive interest rates compared to bank or building society monthly income accounts.

Drawbacks: For maximum benefit you must be willing to hold the bond for at least one year.
Suitable for: Non-taxpayers.

National Savings FIRST Option Bonds

Minimum purchase: £10,000
Maximum purchase: £250,000
Charges: None
Early cash-in penalties: You must hold the bond for a year. If you cash it in during the first year you will get no interest. After a year you can withdraw your bond or reinvest it; there are no top-up purchases.
Interest rates: Fixed at the date you buy. From 6·25% in November 1997.
Special features: Fixed interest rates can be better than other bank or building society accounts.
Drawbacks: You may lose out badly if you have to cash in the bond early.
Suitable for: Lower and basic-rate taxpayers who want to tie up their money for just one year.

National Savings Certificates

Minimum purchase: £100 bought in units of £25.
Maximum purchase: £10,000, but you can reinvest up to £20,000 from previous issues.
Charges: None
Early cash-in penalties: None, although these are intended as a five-year investment. It can take up to two weeks to get your money.
Interest rates: Fixed at the date of issue and tax free. Interest is either paid at the end of the term or when you cash the certificates in. The 44th issue (April 1997) pays 5.35%.
Special features: Tax-free interest
Drawbacks: To get the maximum benefit you must hold the certificate for five years. Make sure you compare interest rates with the best paying TESSAs before committing yourself. Because interest rates are fixed, they are not the best savings if interest rates are rising.
Suitable for: Tax-free status means they are suitable for taxpayers, particularly those who pay higher-rate tax.

National Savings Index-Linked Certificates

Minimum purchase: £100 bought in units of £25.
Maximum purchase: £10,000 but you can reinvest up to £20,000 from previous issues.
Charges: None
Early cash-in penalties: None, although these are intended as a five-year investment. It can take up to two weeks to get your money.
Interest: Tax free at a fixed rate over inflation. The rate you get increases each year. The 11th issue pays an equivalent compound rate of 2·75% plus inflation.
Special features: Tax-free interest at a rate above inflation.
Drawbacks: For maximum benefit you must hold the certificates for five years. You might get a better return with a variable rate TESSA.
Suitable for: Taxpayers, particularly higher-rate taxpayers. If you think inflation will rise quickly in the future it is a good way to protect your savings against inflation erosion.

National Savings Premium Bonds

Minimum purchase: £100
Maximum purchase: £20,000
Charges: None
Early cash-in penalties: You have to hold your bond for a month to be eligible for the prize draw. You can get your money back at any time (in multiples of £10) but you'll have to allow eight days for this.
Interest: No interest is paid on your holdings but you may win tax-free prizes.
Special features: Each month your bonds go into a prize draw until you cash them in.
Drawbacks: You might never win a prize, especially now there are fewer (but bigger prizes). The value of your bonds will gradually be eroded by inflation.
Suitable for: Anyone who likes a bit of a flutter. The odds of you winning a prize draw are greater than winning the lottery. You can always get your money back if you don't win, but as a serious home for your money there are much better alternatives.

Children's Bonus Bonds

Minimum purchase: £25
Maximum holding: £1,000 per issue

Charges: None
Early cash-in penalties: None, except loss of interest
Interest: Fixed over five years. 6·75% in November 1997.
Special features: Returns are tax-free for both children and adults. All the bonds will mature on the bondholder's 21st birthday and even if he or she is already a taxpayer, the interest earned is still tax free. Adults don't pay tax on the interest if they have bought them for children.
Drawbacks: As rates are fixed, you may miss out on better returns elsewhere.
Suitable for: If you want to save for children, Children's Bonus Bonds are definitely worth looking at. Anyone over the age of 16 can buy them on behalf of anyone under the age of 16.

Pensioners Guaranteed Income Bonds

Minimum purchase: £500
Maximum holding: £50,000 per issue
Charges: None
Early cash-in penalties: Full interest is paid after five years. If you want to cash in early you can either give 60 days' notice and earn no interest during that time, or cash in without notice and lose 90 days' interest.
Interest: Fixed over five years. 7% on Series 3.
Special features: Open to anyone aged 60 or over. The interest is paid out as monthly income.
Drawbacks: As with other fixed-interest savings, they are best taken out during periods of low inflation.
Suitable for: Non-taxpayers. The interest is taxable but is deducted at source.

Low- to medium-risk investments

This group includes bonds – of which there is a number of different types. The differences between them relate to the amount of money you can invest and how long it's tied up for. It also includes a specific type of unit trust.

Bonds

There are many investments which are called bonds but which work in very different ways. Premium bonds, National Savings Capital and Income Bonds were covered earlier. Bonds are basically an IOU. In effect, you lend a lump sum to a company which promises to pay you interest over a fixed term, say three, five or ten years. At the end of the term it will give you back your original investment, or at least a guaranteed proportion of it.

You can buy investment bonds through building societies, life insurance companies, investment companies and independent financial advisers. Although the bonds themselves may well invest in a mixture of equities, they are generally less risky than investing directly in the stockmarket, especially if you have the guarantee that you won't lose your capital.

Suitable for: Bonds are generally suitable investments if you're a traditional building society investor looking for a better return without high stockmarket risk. This guide to different types of bond should help you identify which ones might be suitable in your case, according to whether or not you're looking for income or growth.

Convertible bonds

These are fixed-interest securities which can be converted into the shares of the company which issues them. When you take out the bond the terms and time of the conversion are agreed. With a convertible bond you'll get a higher yield than you would with ordinary shares and if the company's share price rises over the life of the bond, you'll enjoy capital growth.
Available through: Investment managers, IFAs
Charges: None.
Minimum investment: Depends on bond.
Maximum investment: Depends on bond.
Interest rates: From around 6%.
Life of bond: Usually five to ten years.
Investment type: Lump sum.
Risk rating: Depends. Smaller companies will offer higher interest rates to attract investors but may be riskier.

Corporate bonds

You place a lump sum with a company. It promises to pay you a fixed rate of interest for the life of the bond and then repay you your original investment at the end of the term. Corporate bonds invest specifically in a collection of bonds, debentures and loan stock which can be traded on the stockmarket.You can hold corporate bonds in a Personal Equity Plan (PEP), which means the returns will be tax free (see page 142). Corporate bond prices rely on interest rates so if rates fall then bond prices rise in value. The opposite is also true.
Available through: Investment managers, IFAs.
Charges: 0·5%–5% initially plus an annual management charge of between 0·7% and 1% depending on the investment.
Minimum investment: £25 a month or lump sum of £500.
Maximum investment: In a PEP £500 a month or £6,000 a year.
Life of bond: Depends on bond. No penalty for instant access.
Interest rates: 8% gross
Investment type: Monthly saving or lump sum.
Risk rating: Because the bond depends on fluctuating interest rates there may be some risk to capital and income.

Distribution bonds

Your lump sum is taken by a life insurance company and invested in a mixture of equities, fixed-interest and index-linked stock, convertibles and cash. Different bonds have different investment mixes. You can draw income on a monthly, six-monthly or annual basis. You may also have the opportunity to reinvest the income.
Available through: Life insurance companies
Charges: Around 5% bid-to-offer spread plus a 1% annual management fee.
Minimum investment: Depends on bond, but it is usually £5,000.
Maximum investment: Depends on bond but there is usually no limit.
Interest rates: 5·8% gross.
Life of bond: Varies. You may incur a penalty charge if you withdraw your money before five years.
Investment type: Lump sum
Risk rating: Because of the investment mix, there can be a risk to capital and income.

Escalator bonds

You put a lump sum on deposit and the interest you get back increases over the term of the bond – hence its name. You will probably have to tie up your money for at least five years and the interest rate will rise by a fixed amount every six to 12 months to keep ahead of inflation. Interest is usually paid once a year.

If you want to take a monthly income option you will have to pay as much as 0.5% below the annual interest rate.

Available through: Life companies, building societies.
Charges: None.
Minimum investment: £1,000.
Maximum investment: £50,000.
Interest rates: Can rise from 5% in year one to 10% in year five.
Life of bond: Usually five years.
Investment type: Lump sum.
Risk: Very low.

Government bonds (or gilts)

These are better known as Government stock or gilts (short for gilt-edged securities). They are loan stocks issued by the government to raise money. As with other bonds, you are promised a fixed rate of interest (known as the coupon) for a set term and then the return of your money at the end of that term, known as the redemption date. Gilts are traded on the stockmarket and their rates rely on fluctuating interest rates. If interest rates fall, gilt prices rise in value and vice versa. You are normally paid interest twice a year, net of basic rate tax. If you're a non-taxpayer you can claim this back.

The nominal, or par, value of each gilt stock is £100. This is the amount you will get back if you hold the gilt to maturity. But as gilts can be bought and sold in the stockmarket, just like shares, their prices can fluctuate above and below par during their lives. If the price of the gilt is higher than par when you buy, you will not get all your capital back on maturity.

The coupon is the interest rate you get on the nominal value of the stock. It is not the same as the interest yield, which takes into account that the gilt price may be above or below par. If it is above par, the interest yield will be lower than the coupon and vice versa.

Gilts are categorised according to number of years they have left to run before they mature. Short-dated gilts, or Shorts, have five years or less to run, medium-dated gilts have five to 15 years left, and long-dated gilts, or Longs, have at least 15 years to run. Some gilts are index-linked, which means that the interest and capital payments are adjusted to compensate for inflation. Others, such as War Loan and some Consolidated Stock, have no redemption at all.

They are very safe, if unspectacular, investments because the government has never failed to meet any interest or capital payments over hundreds of years. There are some risks attached. You can lose money if you have to sell the gilts before they mature and the price has fallen since you bought them. Alternatively, there is the chance of capital growth if the price has risen. Gilts are adverseley affected by stockmarket crashes, but they tend to fall less dramatically and so offer a good defence if a crash is looking likely.

You can buy gilts through a stockbroker, bank, or by post through the National Savings Stock Register (NSSR). The advantage of going through the NSSR is that the interest, although taxable, is paid without tax deducted (gross). This means non-taxpayers don't have to go through the rigmarole of reclaiming tax. Taxpayers, on the other hand, must declare the interest to the Inland Revenue. Interest on gilts held on the Bank of England Register is paid with tax deducted (net).

Available through: Stockbrokers, National Savings Stock Register (NSSR) at post offices, gilt and fixed income unit trusts.
Charges: None except brokers' commission.
Minimum investment: £100.
Maximum investment: No limit.
Interest rates: From around 7%.
Life of bond: Depends, usually between five, ten and fifteen years.
Investment type: Lump sum.
Risk: Some risk as gilt prices depend on fluctuating interest rates.

GUARANTEED INCOME AND GROWTH BONDS

These bonds invest in a mix of stocks and shares, index-linked stocks, convertibles, fixed-interest, cash and gilts. The capital and the rate of interest is guaranteed but rates are not always good. If you go for an income bond you can opt for a monthly income while growth bonds will pay out at the end of the term. You may not be able to get at your money until the bond matures and one

of the major drawbacks of the bond is that basic-rate tax is deducted at source and you can't reclaim it even if you're a non-taxpayer.
Available through: Life insurance companies.
Charges: None.
Interest rates: Around 6% for income bonds; from 8% for growth bonds.
Minimum investment: £1,000.
Maximum investment: £50,000.
Life of bond: One to ten years.
Investment type: Lump sum.
Risk rating: Very low.

Guaranteed stockmarket bonds

The main advantage of these bonds is that they can offer the benefits of stockmarket growth but with much less risk attached. Between 90% and 95% of your investment is placed on deposit to make sure that your capital will be returned to you. The remaining capital is then invested in option contracts to give the investment return. You will usually be given a guaranteed minimum return of, say, 40% on your investment over the life of the bond. Other guarantees may link the return to the rise in the FT-SE 100 index.
Available through: Building societies.
Charges: 0% to 5% of your original investment.
Interest rates: Up to 40% after five years.
Minimum investment: Depends, usually £5,000.
Maximum investment: Up to £250,000.
Life of bond: 3.5 years to 5.5 years.
Investment type: Lump sum.
Risk rating: Very low.

High income bonds

These bonds invest in a similar mix of stockmarket investments to guaranteed income and growth bonds but they will only guarantee the income you'll receive. There are no guarantees to return all your original investment at the end of the term. Some bonds will link their guarantee to stockmarket indices, such as the FT-SE 100. If they have fallen over the time your money is invested you will get back your original capital but minus the total income you have

taken over the investment period.
Available through: Life insurance companies.
Charges: None.
Interest rates: Around 8%.
Minimum investment: £5,000 to £10,000.
Maximum investment: No limit.
Life of bond: Usually five years.
Investment type: Lump sum.
Risk rating: Your capital is at risk.

WITH-PROFITS BONDS

These bonds invest in a mix of equities, fixed-interest, cash, index-linked stock and convertibles to produce capital growth. Maturity dates are often open-ended but most people invest in them for at least five years because cashing them in early can incur quite stiff penalties, especially in the first year. Returns are made through bonus rates, which are declared retrospectively each year. You are not guaranteed that there will be a return but if a bonus rate is declared it can't be taken away from you. You can take regular income on some with-profits bonds.
Available from: Investment managers, life companies.
Charges: Bid-to-offer spread, usually 5% to 6%.
Interest: Paid in the form of non-guaranteed returns, which currently average between 6% and 8%. (CHECK)*
Minimum investment: £2,000 to £10,000.
Maximum investment: Up to £250,000.
Life of bond: People usually invest in them for five to ten years.
Investment type: Lump sum.
Risk rating: Your capital is at risk and returns are not guaranteed.

Cash unit trusts

UNIT TRUSTS ARE COVERED in more detail on page 164. Cash unit trusts work in the same way as conventional unit trusts in that they pool investors' money, but invest in the stockmarket rather than bank and building society deposits. Because they are putting in a great deal more money than the ordinary investor, they can demand much higher interest rates.

You have to pay basic-rate tax on a cash unit trust and the advertised yields you see will be gross, so remember you would have to deduct tax to get the real return. You can't avoid the tax by putting your cash unit trust into a PEP because they don't qualify for inclusion. Cash unit trusts will pay out an income, either quarterly or half yearly.

Available through: Investment managers.

Charges: Initial charges of 0% to 2.5%, annual management charge of 0.5%.

Interest rates: Around 4% after tax.

Minimum investment: From £250 to £5,000 initial investment, depending on the fund. But you can add smaller amounts of £20 to £250 after this.

Maximum investment: No limit.

Risk ratings: Low risk, although there can be small fluctuations in the capital values of the trusts.

Suitable for: Good for investors who want to move out of equities for a limited period. With some investment companies, you can move into their cash unit trusts from equities without incurring any charges. A good alternative to building society accounts in the short and long term.

Medium- to high-risk investments

SOME STOCKMARKET-LINKED investments can be seen as medium risk – non-specialist unit trusts and investment trusts can be suitable for first-time stockmarket investors.

Unit trusts and investment trusts

IF YOU WANT TO spread your risk and avoid direct investment in shares, there are investments which pool investors' money and buy baskets of shares across different sectors and companies. This is something that as a single investor you're unlikely to be able to achieve to the same degree.

You can invest almost anywhere in the world from solid UK companies, such as BT or Marks & Spencer, to companies in developing regions, such as Latin America or the Far East. You can choose to invest in a single country or in a region which comprises several countries. You can also specialise in certain sectors, such as industry or mining, for example. Some of these are riskier than others (see page 175 for information on high-risk sectors).

With unit trusts you can invest in other funds, such as bond funds, which specialise in fixed-interest securities such as corporate bonds, gilts or cash. There are also specialist unit trust funds which buy futures, options or warrants (complex financial contracts which give you the right to buy shares at a future date). You can also invest in unit trusts which invest in investment trusts, or investment trusts which invest in investment trusts. The range is almost endless. See the checklist on pages 166–7.

Although unit trusts and investment trusts invest according to similar principles, the way they operate is different.

Unit trusts

A unit trust is a pooled fund of investors' money which is used to buy shares. If you buy into a unit trust you become a unitholder. You are then entitled to shares in the assets of that trust, equivalent to the number of units you hold. The unit trust is managed by fund managers.

A unit trust is known as an open-ended fund and this is one of the major differences between unit trusts and investment trusts. What this means is that the fund is split into units and the price is set by the fund manager. If lots of people want to buy into the fund then more units are created and the fund gets bigger. If lots of people sell their units, the fund gets smaller. Therefore, the price at which you buy unit trusts is always a true reflection of the value of the fund, known as the net asset value. This can be particularly bad if a lot of people sell their units because the fund not only shrinks but its value is decreased by the loss of investment.

Individual unit trusts concentrate on specific investment areas and so are grouped into different sectors – according to geographic areas, or whether the fund managers concentrate on growth or on generating income. Some invest in other unit trusts – these are called funds of funds.

There are also 'tracker funds'. These track stockmarket indices, such as the FT-SE 100, and shares are chosen according to a complex computer formula to reflect what is happening in the stockmarket. Very few fund managers have managed to outperform the stockmarket index over a long period of time, which is why index tracker funds can seem so attractive.

Available through: Investment managers, IFAs.

Charges: Initial charges are based on the bid-to-offer spread: between 3% and 5% of the fund's value. You will also have to pay an annual management charge of around 1.5% of the fund's value.

Minimum investment: Lump sum: £500. Savings schemes: From £20 a month.

Maximum investment: If your unit trust is wrapped in a PEP, you can only invest a maximum of £6,000 a year or £500 a month. Otherwise, no maximum limits.

Length of investment: You should see this as at least a medium- to long-term investment (five years or longer).

Investment type: Lump sum or monthly savings.

Risk rating: Depends on what you invest in. UK blue chips will be much less risky than Latin American emerging markets. But because you are investing in equities, there will always be some risk to your capital.

Suitable for: Most investors. There are a range of funds which suit everybody. If you are risk averse, a unit trust is often a better choice than an investment trust because there are more unit trusts which specialise in UK blue chip companies. You can invest for both income and capital growth.

INVESTMENT TRUSTS

An investment trust is a public limited company and its shares are quoted on the stock exchange. Because it is a company, the trust has a board of directors and when you buy shares, you have a say in how the trust is managed, in much the same way as normal shareholders have a say in how their company is run.

Investment trusts are known as closed-ended funds. This means that the number of shares which can be bought and sold

Picking a trust checklist

1 Work out your attitude to risk
This will depend on several factors:

- How much you have to invest: The less you have, the less you can afford to lose.
- How long you want to invest for: If you can invest for 25 years then you can afford to take more risk because your investment will have more time to make a recovery if it falls at any point. If you want to see a return in five years, then choose something safer.
- How you feel about risk: If you're worried about taking a high risk, then don't.

2 Choose the sector you want to invest in
This depends on your attitude to risk and how much you have to invest.

- If you have a large lump sum to invest you might want to invest in more than one sector.
- If you are new to investing, you might want to choose a safe investment, such as gilt or corporate bond unit trusts.
- Large, well-spread funds across many countries, for example, Europe, generally have a lower level of risk and are a good way for you to start investing in the stockmarket.
- If you want to take a high risk you should take a look at emerging markets, single countries, smaller companies or venture capital trusts (see page 175)

3 Look at performance
Before you make your choice, find out how the trusts have performed over the past one, five and ten years. Don't rely on the figures you read in advertisements. Don't automatically choose the current top ten performers. They may have had a short spell of good performance, but they could easily dip. However, you should always pick trusts with above-average performance.

There are different benchmarks you can use to check performance. These include the Retail Price Index, the market index, such as the FT-SE 100, Hoare Govett Smaller Companies, or the Morgan Stanley International Index. Before you buy a unit trust find out which benchmarks the fund manager uses and how successful the manager is according to these figures.

Remember that the trust you choose is prey to constant fluctuations in the stockmarkets; if the markets are falling sharply, then so will the value of your investment. This is why it is better to invest for the medium to long term so that your trust will have time to weather the ups and downs of the stockmarket.

4 Objectives and philosophy

Different funds will have different objectives and different fund managers have different ideas about the way to pick stock.

Find out what strategy for investing the fund manager uses. The two main strategies are top-up investment, which relies on the fund manager's ability to pick winning stocks, and top-down investment, where a team of specialists decide what strategy to adopt and then pick stocks from a recommended list. Either philosophy can work, but some experts feel that the top-down philosophy has a better chance of consistent performance.

5 Decide what you want from your trust

If you want an income from your investment you will need to go for a high-yielding trust.

Find out how often dividend payments are made. They could be paid annually, twice yearly, quarterly or monthly.

Decide whether you want to put in a lump sum or save monthly, and find out how much the minimum investment is for the trust.

Look at the other funds that the investment company operates and find out how well managed they are. If, over time, your fund does not perform as well as you had hoped then you may be able to switch to another fund within the group. Some investment companies will also charge a discount if you decide to switch to a fund within another group.

6 Look at the charges

Charges vary between trusts so you need to make sure that you understand them. If you don't, get an IFA or fund manager to explain them to you before you make any decisions.

Some funds may charge exit charges. These are put in place to discourage you from taking your money out too early.

If you invest in gilt and bond unit trusts, for example, you will probably pay much lower charges than if you invest in equity funds.

Look for a fund which has a low bid-to-offer spread if you can. This is the difference between the buying and selling prices. You will pay higher charges if you invest in a trust which specialises in smaller companies or emerging markets, because such trusts usually have wider bid-to-offer spreads.

7 Once you've chosen your fund

Don't forget about it. Check on it from time to time to make sure that its performance isn't slipping. If performance does slip, don't bail out too quickly. It could be a blip and if you've chosen well your investment should make a recovery. Read the financial press and *Moneywise* to keep abreast of what's happening in the markets.

within the fund is already fixed and people buy and sell the shares according to the market value on the day. Because the price of the shares fluctuates, they can vary above or below the value of the fund. When the shares are above the value of the fund they are said to be trading at a premium. When they are below, they are said to be trading at a discount. An investment trust trading at a discount is obviously good news if you are buying into the fund, but not so good if you are wanting to sell your shares. Conversely, if the trust is trading at a premium it is not good news if you want to buy in.

Only investment trusts are allowed to borrow money to invest on behalf of fund members. This is known as gearing. This means that more money is invested for you when share prices are rising, boosting your investment, but it also exaggerates the losses when share prices are falling.

Like unit trusts, investment trusts are grouped according to the area or objective of investment in which they specialise. Some investment trusts offer a variety of different types of share giving different types of return. Broadly speaking, some of them offer an income but no capital growth and others the opposite. These are called split capital investment trusts.

Available through: Investment managers, IFAs.

Charges: You are effectively buying and selling shares, so you pay dealing costs based on the broker's commission, stamp duty and the Panel on Takeovers and Mergers (PTM) levy. These vary from about 0% to 3% of the value of your investment. In addition, you'll have to pay annual management charges of around 0.25% and 0.5% of the value of the assets.

Minimum investment: Around £250 lump sum, £30 monthly savings scheme.

Maximum investment: If you wrap your investment trust in a tax-free PEP, you can invest £6,000 a year or £500 a month.

Early redemption penalties: None, you can cash in your investment when you want.

Length of investment: You should see investment trusts as a medium- to long-term investment, (at least five years).

Investment type: Lump sum or investment savings.

Risk ratings: This depends on what you invest in. Investment trusts have the reputation for being more risky than unit trusts but if you want to take a medium risk there is little to choose between unit and investment trusts. If you want to take a high risk, investment trusts can be better placed for long-term planning in the high-risk markets, such as emerging markets, or venture capital companies. This is because investment trust companies are much less dependent on a constant flow of liquid assets to keep the fund afloat. And because their capital is fixed they are in a much better position to take a long-term view of the market. You really need stability if you are going to deal with volatile markets.

Suitable for: Medium- to high-risk investors, but don't write off investment trusts if you are risk-averse. There are some low-risk funds and investment trusts which have historically showed better returns than unit trusts.

Open-ended investment companies

Open-ended investment companies or OEICs (pronounced Oiks) were only launched in 1997. These type of investments are already popular in Europe and they are intended to attract more money from countries in the European Union.

OEICs are really a hybrid of unit trusts and investment trusts because they are open-ended like unit trusts, so that the size of the fund expands and contracts as people buy in or sell out. On the other hand they are quoted companies like investment trusts. The way in which OEICs do differ from unit trusts and investment trusts, is in the way they behave. In unit trusts the segments you invest in are known as units, while with OEICs they will be known as shares.

One of the advantages of OEICs should be their pricing structure. The shares will only reflect the net asset value of the fund (unlike investment trusts, see page 165), so the price can only move up or down in relation to the real value of the fund. OEICs will also only have one pricing structure so the price you buy or sell at will be the same. With unit trusts there is a different price for buying and selling known as the bid-to-offer spread. There is the price that you pay to buy the units (the offer price) and the lower price you are paid when you sell the units (the bid price). The bid-to-offer spread is usually incorporated in the fund manager's charges and can be up to 5% of your investment. Single pricing may come into effect for unit trusts in the future, but in the meantime, this should mean that if you invest in an OEIC you will pay lower charges.

You may also get a better deal on the shares you buy because the OEIC regulations allow fund managers to offer different and perhaps cheaper classes of shares. Many OEICs aim to run umbrella funds, so that if your investment aims change you should be able to switch to a more suitable fund. As there are very few funds in existence it is too soon to say what impact they will have on the UK onshore investment market (they have been available offshore for years) but they should appeal to you if you already invest in unit trusts or investment trusts and want to look at another product.

Permanent interest-bearing shares

BUILDING SOCIETY RETURNS are safe but unspectacular. (See page 149 for more on building society accounts.) But if you want to get a better return for your money from a building society you could consider permanent interest bearing shares (known as PIBS).

PIBS are basically loans to the building society. Minimum deposits can be high: from £1,000 to £10. In return for loaning it the money, the building society will pay you a fixed rate of interest twice a year for as long as you hold the shares.

Although PIBS are issued by building societies, you buy them through a stockbroker because they are listed and traded like other shares. They are always issued at 100p a share but their price is affected by two things: how well the issuing building society is doing and, because the interest paid on PIBS is fixed, how interest rates are doing. If interest rates are low, a high fixed rate is obviously attractive, but if interest rates climb then it becomes less desirable and the price may fall below 100p.

When you see PIBS listed in the financial pages, there will be columns headed 'fixed gross coupon', 'Buying price' and 'Gross yield'. These can help you work out how much you can sell your PIBS for and what your return will be – the real gross yield. To work out the real gross yield you need to multiply the fixed gross interest rate (listed as the fixed gross coupon) by £100 and divide that figure by the market price. So for example, the real gross yield of a PIBS with a coupon of 12% and a price of £126.15p would be (12 x 100)/126.15 which would give a real gross yield of 9.51%.

Available through: Stockbrokers.

Charges: Normal stockbroker dealing charges, around 1.5% on £5,000.

Interest rates: Fixed, paying around 7·7% as this book was being published.

Minimum investment: Depends on the building society. £1,000 to £50,000.

Maximum investment: No limit. (CHECK)

Length of investment: No limit.

Investment type: Lump sum.

Risk rating: PIBS do have some risks attached. Their value can fall, particularly when interest rates are high. You aren't guaranteed your money back because the issuing society does not have to pay back the nominal value of the shares. If the building society misses an interest payment it does not have to make it up later. If a building society goes bust you are at the back of the queue for any handout of assets. PIBs are not covered by the Building Societies Investor Protection Fund so you don't get any compensation if anything goes wrong. Risks of building societies failing are small.

Suitable for: Older investors planning for retirement and people with a lump sum to invest. The interest on PIBS is paid net of basic rate tax but if you are a non-taxpayer you can reclaim part or all of the tax. Generally you do not pay capital gains tax if you sell at a profit. You may also qualify for a windfall if the building society floats.

Investment-linked life insurance

INVESTMENT-LINKED LIFE INSURANCE plans used to be popular investments, particularly as endowment policies linked to mortgages. However, reports of endowment polices failing to grow enough to pay off people's mortgages, added to high penalties for early surrender, has meant endowment policies have fallen out of favour.

Life insurance plans are basically savings plans that offer built-in life insurance. They are long-term investments bought through life insurance companies. The minimum term you can take one out for is usually ten years but many run for 25 or 30 years. You pay regular premiums into your policy which are then invested for you by the life insurance company into shares, Government stocks, property and other investments. At the end of your agreed term you will be paid a lump sum. If you die before the policy matures, your dependants will receive the amount for which your life is insured, known as the sum assured. There are many types of savings plan apart from endowment policies, including some bonds, such as guaranteed income bonds (see page 160).

THREE MAIN TYPES OF POLICY:

- *With-profits*: The most popular form of policy. Growth is provided by a series of bonuses paid each year by the insurance company. The bonuses are calculated to weather the ups and downs of the investment's performance so, in a good year, some of the value of the bonus may be held back to add to a bonus in a year when performance is poor. Once the insurance company has awarded the bonus it can't take it away again. Often a large portion of the final sum can be made up by a terminal bonus which can be as much as a quarter of the fund's value, which is why it is worth persevering to the end of the policy's life.
- *Unit-linked*: With this policy, the value directly reflects the value of its investments, so it can fluctuate more widely than a

Endowment policies

If you decide to take out an endowment policy follow a few simple rules:

- Think carefully about whether it is the best vehicle for you to pay off a mortgage. There are many more flexible mortgage products on the market now (see Chapter 5) and if you need life insurance you can buy it cheaply as a stand-alone policy (see Chapter 6).

- Decide whether you are prepared to commit yourself to save for the full term of the policy. Early surrender penalties (within the first five years) can be punitive, leaving you severely out of pocket. Also, the final lump sum you get might be greatly enhanced by a terminal bonus paid when the policy matures. On a ten-year policy this could be over a quarter of the final value. On a 25-year policy it could be well over half the value.

- You must be prepared to save for the life of the policy and this could mean a commitment of at least ten years, if not 25. Are your circumstances secure enough to meet this commitment? If you are worried you may not be able to manage, look at shorter term savings plans, such as TESSAs, which lock up your money for five years, or PEP savings plans, which you can stop and start at will.

with-profits policy. If the markets are doing well then so will your policy. If they fall, you can lose a lot of money.

- *Unitised with-profits*: This policy falls between the security of a with-profits policy and the vagaries of a unit-linked policy. It will track the ups and downs of investment markets but will offer some protection against you losing out too heavily if markets fall.

If you use a life insurance savings plan as a straightforward savings scheme, rather than a vehicle for paying off your mortgage, you might be pleasantly surprised; because you are not relying on it to perform to a level guaranteed to provide you with enough money, you remove the worry that this might not happen. The top performing ten-year endowment policy gave an annual yield of almost 10%, which is a far better yield than you would have got in a building society over the same term.
Available through: Life insurance companies
Minimum deposit: £10 to £100 a month
Maximum deposit: No limit, except on some with-profit bonds.

Charges: Yes and they can be punitive if you cash in your investment early.
Suitable for: Good for higher-rate taxpayers. You can avoid paying higher-rate tax with a qualifying or non-qualifying savings plan and you can save as much as you want each month. This is because life companies pay basic rate income tax and capital gains tax on the income and profits they make on investments, so policyholders don't have to pay any more tax if they belong to a qualifying plan. A policy is termed qualifying if you pay premiums at least once a year. If you surrender a policy or make it paid up (see below) it will be treated as qualifying.
Risk rating: If you cash the policy in during the first ten years, it may not be treated as qualifying and you may have to pay higher-rate tax. Investment-linked insurance savings plans are generally not suitable for non-taxpayers. If you're a basic-rate taxpayer make use of your PEP and TESSA allowances before investing in a plan.

Traded endowment policies

Even with careful financial planning, you may find yourself in a situation where you have to surrender an endowment policy, through divorce or redundancy, for example. If this happens, it may be worthwhile looking at selling your endowment policy to a company that buys and sells second-hand policies rather than surrendering it to the life insurance company.

An alternative to trading your policy is to make it paid up. This means that you stop paying in premiums and the insurance company then reduces the guaranteed sum for which you are insured. This new figure, the paid-up value, is then paid out to you when the policy matures or to your heirs if you die. You may still continue to have bonuses added to your fund, even though you are no longer paying premiums.

If your policy has been running for at least six years and has a surrender value of at least £2,000 you should be able to trade it. You should get around 10% to 15% more than you would by surrendering it to an insurance company. The closer it is to maturity the better deal you'll get.

You can also invest in traded endowment policies, which can be particularly attractive if you take on a policy mid-term and see it through to its maturity value, because you will qualify for the terminal bonus. However, you should only do this if you know you will be able to stick with the payments until the policy has matured.

FRIENDLY SOCIETY POLICIES

You can also take out similar products to those offered by life insurance companies with friendly societies. Their main advantage is that unlike life insurance plans, the money grows in the fund tax free and you won't pay any tax when the policy matures and you collect your lump sum.

You can only invest £25 a month into a friendly society plan or £270 a year to qualify for tax-free status CHECK. Watch out for policies with higher premiums than this as you may not get tax exemption on the whole amount and may be better off investing in a PEP or TESSA.

High-risk investments

THIS GROUP IS NOT for the fainthearted! If you're hoping to invest some money you might need at a specific time, steer clear of these investments. But if you've money you can afford to lose and leave invested for the long term, high risk can mean high reward.

Unit trusts and investment trusts

THE PREVIOUS CHAPTER covered the way these investments work in detail. The investments held by some trusts mean they should be classed as high risk:

- *Emerging markets*: These are countries whose economies are growing rapidly but whose equity markets are fairly new. The Far East, Latin America and Eastern Europe are good examples of emerging markets. Their markets can grow at double the rate of established economies, which is reflected in their stockmarket prices, but they are prey to political instability, and overheating economies causing spectacular crashes.

- *Venture capital*: Some investment trusts invest in venture capital projects. Investors put up money for new and sometimes risky projects and because these projects start from a low base they have the potential for huge growth.

Shares

YOU MIGHT ALREADY be a shareholder if you have benefited from the latest round of demutualising building society payouts. Over 20 million new shareholders were created in 1997 alone with the flotation of the Halifax, Alliance & Leicester, Woolwich and Northern Rock building societies. Alternatively, you may hold a few shares in the utility companies.

However, there is a big difference between owning a few shares and regularly trading on the stockmarket. Sharedealing can be a risky business and you should not put any more money directly into shares than you can afford to lose. If you are very risk-averse person then regular sharedealing may not be the best option for you, and you may be better off looking at other savings and investments, such as gilts, TESSAs or some bonds (see 'Low-risk investments', starting on page 149) and 'Low- to medium-risk investments', starting on page 159.

If you fancy having a go at investing in the stockmarket but are worried about losing a lot of money then you can spread your risk by investing in unit trusts or investment trusts which buy baskets of shares across lower-risk sectors (see Medium- to high-risk investments on page 163). There are, however, unit trust and investment trusts which deal in specific areas, such as emerging markets. The risks are high but so can be the returns. For more details see page 175.

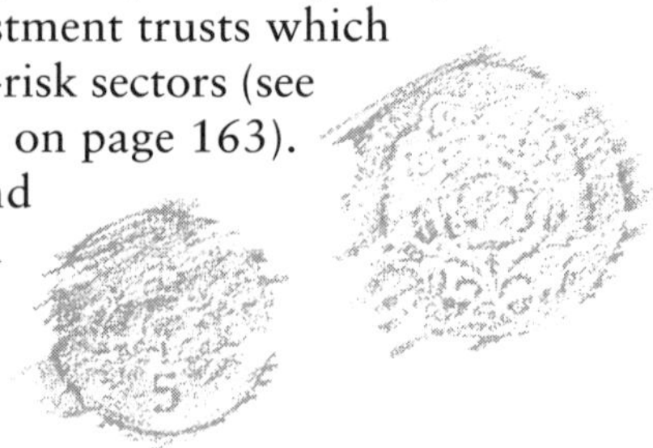

Dealing on the stockmarket

If you still want to deal regularly on the stockmarket, you need to do some research to make sure you know what you are letting yourself in for.

Follow these rules before you start to buy or sell shares:

- Don't spend more than you can afford to lose, and make sure that you have all your necessary financial planning, such as pension, mortgage and your family's long-term protection sorted out first.
- Get to know your markets. This means reading up on the subject and becoming familiar with what is happening, looking at annual reports and going to AGMs if you are already a shareholder.
- Know why you are investing. Do you want income from your shares or are you investing for growth?
- Know your level of risk. Although shares are risky investments, some are more risky than others.
- If you need advice, find a good stockbroker and decide which service you want from the options below.

What sort of shares can I buy?

Ordinary shares
Companies issue shares so that they can raise capital for their business. When you buy an ordinary share you literally buy a small (or large) part of the company, depending on the size of your stake. This means you have the right to benefit from its earnings and profits and that you have a say in how the company is run. You usually make your views heard at the annual general meeting (AGM).

High-yielding shares
Some shares have high yields and they can be better bets than putting your money into gilts or fixed-income bonds because the shares may still continue to rise in value.

Advantages of owning them: They are less risky than growth stocks (see below) because they are not expected to grow so quickly so any setbacks will have less of an impact on share prices.

Growth stocks

Investors are looking for an upward movement in the share price rather than a high dividend yield. Growth companies are usually those in expanding market sectors. In addition, they will benefit from good management, have higher than average profits and be at a stage where they want to plough profits back in to expand the business further. You can therefore expect that the dividend yield will be lower and the price/earnings ratio will be higher (see page 180).

Advantages of owning them: Growth companies can offer spectacular returns. Because you receive a lower income and a higher capital gain, as long as the capital gains are less than £6,500 they will be tax free.

Recovery stocks

These are shares of companies which are going through a rough patch. They may be firms that are well managed but have seen a drop in profits because the general market is poor, or they may be companies which have not met investors' expectations or are failing.

Advantages of owning them: If you buy these shares at the end of a recession, say, or when they have hit the bottom of their cycle you could benefit when they start to pick up again. Conversely, they may not manage to do that and the price will fall further. You need to know a lot about the companies concerned and the chances that they will recover before you invest.

Blue chip shares

The term comes from the stakes in poker and it refers to shares which are often issued by big companies and household names. These companies will be probably valued at a minimum of £5bn and form the basis of many pension funds and insurance company portfolios. Most blue chip shares will fall into the FT-SE 100 which lists the top 100 companies in the UK.

Advantages of owning them: Large companies are unlikely to go bust, and you will be able to track their movements easily because a lot is written about them in the press. You can do your own research as to whether they are worth buying. If the carpark is fuller at Tesco than at Sainsbury's, maybe now is the time to move your money into Tesco shares!

Smaller company shares
As the name suggests, these are shares which invest in smaller companies. Small can be a misnomer. To qualify as a smaller company, the company must be valued at between £20m and £150m. Smaller companies are often listed on the Alternative Investment Market (AIM) list in the share pages of the *Financial Times.*

Advantages of owning them: Smaller company shares have historically outperformed the blue chip shares, but they have not been so successful in the 1990s although the trend looks set to pick up by the year 2000.

If you are prepared to do your research on smaller companies you could become an expert on the market. Large pension funds and insurance companies tend to ignore smaller companies because the impact of their growth is too small. Fund managers may also stay away from them unless the fund is specifically in smaller companies, because they tend to be riskier propositions. But remember that today's smaller company could be tomorrow's blue chip giant.

Penny shares
So named because all they cost is a few pennies. They are shares from companies at the absolute bottom of their cycle, whose profits have fallen to rock bottom, or whose profits have simply stagnated. The gamble you take is that they are going to find their feet and rise again. Of course, this may not happen and you may suffer even greater losses. You want to take into account the bid-to-offer spread (the difference between the buying and selling price). If this is large you may not even get your money back until the shares have started to move up a lot further.

Advantages of owning them: They can be fun but they are risky. You have the potential to make a huge profit.

When to buy and sell shares

Does the share fit your portfolio? It may look a good price but don't weight your investments too much into one sector or company.

The financial ratios

- *The dividend yield*:This shows how much you will receive in dividends or a share of the company profits. Dividends are taxed and you usually receive them twice a year. They are normally paid by cheque. Dividends are important because they are also used to work out the yield of shares. The yield is the dividend expressed as a percentage of the share price. If you buy a share for £1 which has a 5p dividend, the yield on your share will be 5%. But if the share price rises to £2, the yield will halve. If the share price fell to 50p the yield would rise to 10%. It is essential to work out the dividend yield if income is a reason for investing.

- *The price/earnings ratio*: It's not enough to look at the profits of a company. If you had a choice between investing in two companies which each made £1m profit, it would be better to invest in the company that issued £5m shares than the one that issued £10m. This is because the earnings per share will be higher. If you're looking at a company you need to assess its earnings per share. To do this you divide the after tax profits by the number of shares issued.

Once you have this figure you can work out the price/earnings (p/e) ratio. The p/e ratio is the share price divided by the earnings per share. This figure will give you a rough idea of how long it would take your stake to be paid back in full, so a p/e of 10 will take 10 years.

Although you would think that a low p/e ratio would be better, the company must be in good financial shape if it only takes, say, four years to pay back the investment, the opposite is true. Companies which are doing well tend to have higher share prices and therefore higher p/e ratios because the markets expect that they will continue to increase their profits.

Look at the share price movements over the short term as this will give you the best indication as to whether your investment is worth buying. Don't buy into a downward moving share unless you are pretty confident that the price is going to start moving up again.

Once you've bought your shares, make sure you monitor the share price closely so that you are aware of what your investment is doing. If you were buying the shares for a reason such as an anticipated takeover, and then that

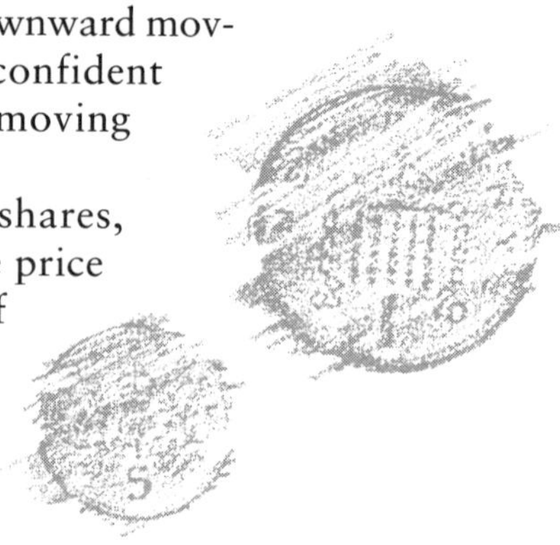

takeover really happens, work out whether you would still buy the shares at their new value. If the price has fallen then you should probably sell; if the price has risen, work out the likelihood of it rising further before you make a move.

Look at the general market place. Your share price might be stable now, but make sure you are aware of any factors that might eventually influence its price. If you are unsure why you are holding a share, or if it no longer fits into your investment portfolio, you should sell. Always sell shares before they hit the very top, otherwise you might lose out when they start to fall.

How to buy and sell shares

You need to decide on the type of service you want – essentially whether you want advice or whether you want to be able to make all the buying and selling decisions on your own.

Execution-only service

If you want to buy and sell shares, the stockbroker simply carries out your instructions without offering you any advice. You will then only pay a dealing fee. This is the cheapest way to buy and sell shares.

Portfolio management service

If you have a number of shares (known as a portfolio), the stockbroker will look after your portfolio and suggest whether you should buy or sell certain shares but it is up to you to make the final decisions. If you are new to share buying and selling, this service might be helpful.

Discretionary management service

If you opt for this service, the broker will buy and sell shares for you without waiting for your permission. The stockbroker will also offer you other services, such as portfolio valuations or working out your capital gains tax liabilities.

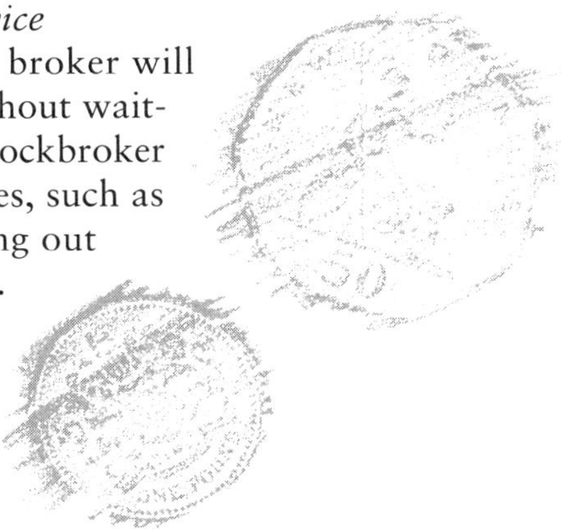

Most sharedealing services are carried out either over the phone or by post. All you have to do is ring or write to your broker instructing him or her what you want to buy or sell. You should give specific instructions, such as how many shares you want to buy or sell and what price you are prepared to pay or receive. Once you have given your instructions you can't change your mind because you've made a verbal contract, so think what you want to say before you say it. Dealing charges vary according to the service you've chosen. Execution-only is cheapest, and obviously you pay more if you're getting advice. As a rule of thumb postal services start at around £5 and telephone services from about £8.

Under a system for settling stockmarket deals introduced in July 1994, you have to pay or provide the shares a certain number of days after the deal is struck. As this book was published the number of days was 5 , which is called T + 5, but this was due to change to T + 3. You may still be able to deal for a longer settlement period, but it may cost you more. You don't have to have share certificates any more under a system for 'dematerialising' share dealing introduced in 1996 called CREST. Some brokers will encourage you to hold your shares in their nominee account. You may decide you're happy with this arrangement, but bear in mind you lose your legal status as a shareholder and may have to pay for things you would otherwise have got automatically – company reports and accounts, for example.

New issues

If a company wants to get on to the stockmarket it needs to find an outlet to sell its shares. It usually does this by employing a sponsor, usually a bank or stockbroker, to place an offer for sale on new issue shares. The sponsor does this by placing an advertisement in a newspaper, listing the details of the company and how many shares are for sale and what price they will be. If you are interested you fill in the accompanying application form and send it back with a cheque for the number of shares you want. If the offer is over-subscribed the sponsor will allocate the shares.

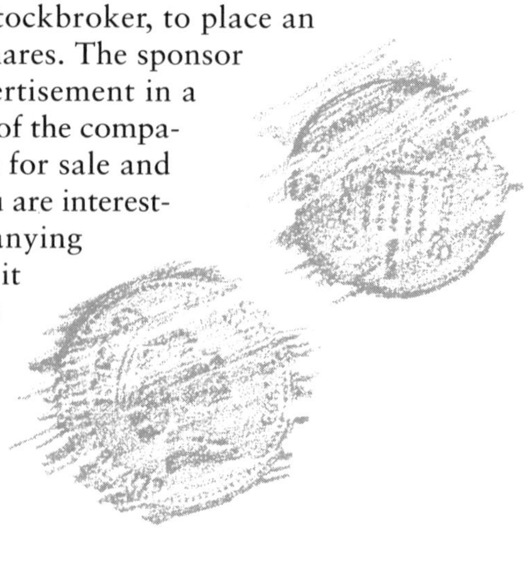

Scrip or bonus issues
If a share price rises sharply, the company may issue free shares to existing shareholders to reduce the value of the shares but not the value of the holding. So, if you had 500 shares in a company that were worth 200p each, your holding would be worth £1,000. If the company offered a one-for-one scrip issue, which means that they would issue one free share for every one you hold, you would increase your shareholding to 1,000 shares but their value would remain at £1,000 and the share price would fall to 100p per share.

Rights issues
If a company wants to raise more money to invest, it may contact its existing shareholders to ask them if they wish to invest more money in exchange for new shares. This is known as making a rights issue.

Any rates of return quoted were typical as this book was published – remember they may have changed.

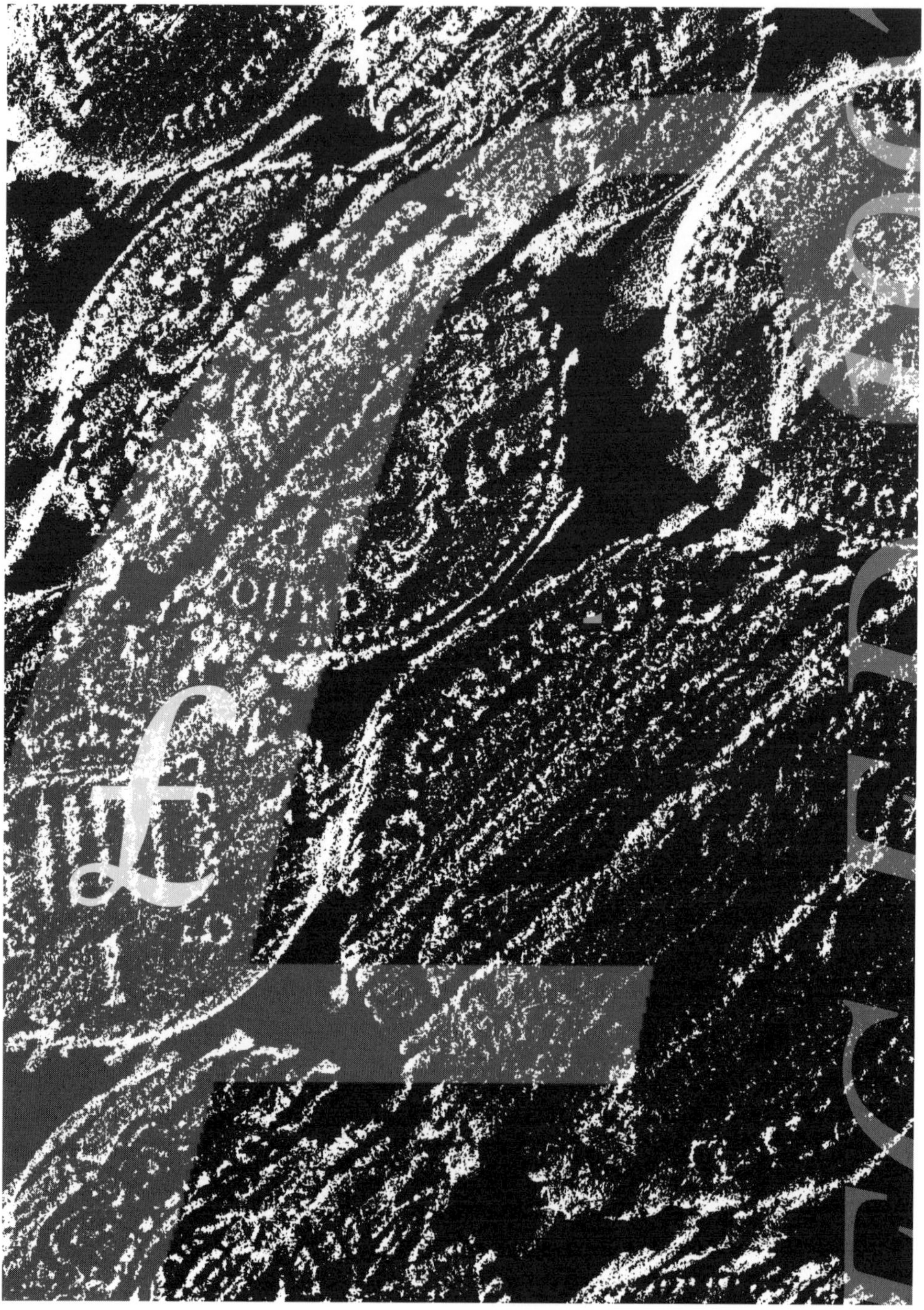

10 Putting your plans into practice

We've already looked at how you can gear your investments towards getting a regular income or allowing them to grow as much as possible, and have considered the options for achieving these targets. However, many of us have a particular goal in mind, such as saving for our children's education or university fees.

In this chapter we show you how you can co-ordinate your investment plans to make sure that they are all useful for your individual goals.

Here are some of the most common investment targets and some ideas on how to combine your investment plans to make sure you reach them.

Saving for children

CHILDREN ARE UNBELIEVABLY EXPENSIVE, but the basic rule of financial planning applies: start early for the best deal. The longer your money has to work for you, the easier it will be to fund your plans, so even if one of your children wants to become an architect (seven years' training), you'll be able to cope.

If you're saving for your own children, then the best thing is to start before they are born, but clearly only the truly financially prudent would do that. When they are born you are likely to get some cash gifts from doting friends and relatives. Resist the urge to spend it all on baby gear – remember, they'll grow out of it very quickly and you can get lots of the basic stuff second-hand. (A copy of Noelle Walsh's *Good Deal Directory* will come in handy in finding bargains). There are two reasons you might be saving for children: one is to build a lump sum for the child's own use, perhaps to teach him or her the value of money and saving, the other is to use money to fund education costs. We'll deal with them separately.

Building a nest egg

As a parent you have to be careful when you save money on behalf of your children. Children have their own tax allowances in the same way as an adult, but any income generated from investments you've made on the child's behalf will be taxed on your income. It's also taxed at your top rate. But your child can earn £200 a year interest (£100 from each parent) before this rule is enforced. Choose tax-free gifts or an investment generating capital gains – such as shares – if you are investing for your own children. Any income the child gets from money invested by family and friends is counted as his or her own, as part of the tax allowance in the normal way.

Low-risk ideas for parents' gifts

- *Bank and building society accounts*: Unexciting, but useful if you want to put all the cash given to your child in one place, plus any child allowance and other cash. You can take out an account in the child's name if you want him or her to have access to the money when he or she is older. There are plenty of Young Savers' accounts available. A lot of them offer gimmicks but not much interest. Get one with a decent interest rate or open one of the better paying postal accounts aimed at adults.
- *National Savings Children's Bonus Bonds*: These roll up tax-free and are guaranteed by the government.
- *Friendly Society savings plans*: You'll often see these advertised in the press. You can only put in £270 a year. They are indeed tax-free, as the advertisements suggest, but you must keep paying into the bond for the full ten-year term. This is because your money is invested in a fund which has extremely high charges in the early years. Friendly Societies offer unit-linked (stockmarket-linked) and with-profits investments (see page 172). The unit-linked funds are riskier but should offer you better results in the long term.
- *Premium Bonds*: The payouts are tax-free but of course there's no guarantee your child will win anything.

Independent financial adviser and *Moneywise* Ask The Professionals panellist Keith Sanham says:

"Financial presents I'd suggest for a new baby are Premium Bonds, a good long-term savings plan with a unit trust or investment trust ... or a lottery ticket!"

You should combine some or all of the above ideas with some element of stockmarket investment. This will give you a better chance of building up your child's capital for the long term. Put your money into unit trusts and investment trusts geared to growth rather than income (see page 163).

Other friends and relatives can give whatever they want. It's useful to ask them to write a note with the gift, such as 'here's £50 for your birthday' so that you can prove the money didn't come from you.

Planning for education costs

Don't ignore this just because you don't intend for your children to go to private school. Parents are already expected to find £1,000 a term towards university tuition fees and this burden is likely to rise in the future.

The way you plan for education depends very much on how much time you have before you'll need the money.

Emergency plans

We get lots of letters from worried parents who feel their child isn't doing well in state school. They are unexpectedly facing the immediate cost of private education. You'll need to find £4,000 a year for a day school (in London up to £10,000 a year), and up to £14,850 a year for a boarder. Here's how to manage the costs:

1 *Are there any discounts available?* The assisted places scheme may be dead but there are a huge range of scholarships and grants. Check with the private schools you have in mind to see what they offer, and have a look at the *Directory of Grant-making Trusts*, which you'll find in the public library. Some charities and trade organisations offer help with fees. If your child is exceptionally bright he or she may be eligible for an academic scholarship, paid regardless of parental income. If you have a small son who can sing, the choir schools offer a unique way into private education. Voice trials usually take place at age seven. Your child will get a prep school education and a full musical training – many choristers go on to win full music scholarships at public schools.

2 *Extend your mortgage*: If you already have some equity in your home you can take out some cash and extend the loan to cover extra payments. (See below for flexible mortgages.)
3 *Pay out of your day-to-day income*: This simply means reviewing your finances and cutting back so that you can afford the fees. You should avoid dipping into your emergency savings if you can, but this might be inevitable. You might be able to get a loan secured on an investment-linked life insurance policy if you have one which is not linked to a mortgage.
4 *Get a flexible mortgage* (see page 77): These new deals allow you to miss several months' payments, or to pay a lump sum into your account and then take it out again if you need the money. Some give customers cheque books and allow you to borrow against the equity you already have in your home. This might be ideal if you aren't already tied to a mortgage with punitive charges for people who switch to another lender.

Planning ahead

You have much more flexibility if you have five years or more to save. Here are some ideas:
1 *TESSAs*: You and your spouse can have a TESSA each, both putting in £9,000. This gives you tax-free growth to fund fees. You can roll up the capital into a second TESSA if you have more than five years before you need the money, and re-invest the interest.
2 *PEPs*: You and your spouse can put £6,000 into a general PEP every year. Choose a growth PEP for long-term investment.
3 *Split-capital investment trusts*: These are often mentioned as a useful tool for people who need to save for education. You buy zero-preference shares in the split-capital trust. These offer a pre-determined rate of growth repaid on a fixed redemption date which allows you to plan ahead. They are tax-efficient because the gain is classed as capital not income and each parent can take the first

> Independent financial adviser and *Moneywise* Ask The Professionals panellist Keith Sanham says:
>
> "Planning for school fees is no different to any other investment strategy. Go for flexibility and accessibility. This does not sit well with educational trusts whose days may well be numbered in any event."

£6,500 of capital gains tax-free.

4 *Endowments and special school fees savings policies*: School fees policies have lost favour in the last few years, but they are basically endowments. You could still take out a with-profits endowment if you wanted a low-risk way to save, with the discipline of regular payments.

5 *Educational trusts*: These used to be popular because of tax breaks but these have now been restricted.

Early retirement

EMPLOYMENT PROSPECTS FOR the over-45s are often grim, so even if you don't plan to swan off on a boat at 55 you must boost your retirement savings as much as you can while you're still working, and aim for an early retirement goal. If you do that then enforced retirement won't hit so hard.

Obviously, retirement at 60 is a much more realistic goal for most of us than 55 or even 50. Women have particular problems: many haven't paid anything like enough pension contributions because they have had career breaks or stopped work altogether when they had children. Divorce or redundancy can hit women especially hard.

Get a projection of how much your pension will be if you retire early, and how much you still have to pay in if you want to retire at 50, 55 or 60 on your chosen income level. You should be able to get a personal pension provider to show you how much shortfall there is. Employers schemes will be able to show you how you are doing plus the effect that buying added years or making extra contributions would have.

Here are some of the best ways to combine investments to boost your funds:

1 *Adding lump sums or regular extra payments to your pension*: Again, the longer the money is invested, the harder it can work. Buying added years in an employers pension scheme, additional voluntary contributions (AVCs) in a company scheme, or free-standing AVCs in an independent fund should help you make the most of your pension. It's worth getting an

independent adviser to sort out how best you could make use of your money. For example, if you've had windfall shares from an ex-building society you might do well to put the money into a pension.

2 *PEPs*: You are only allowed one general PEP and one single-company scheme per financial year, but if there are two of you and you both take out PEPs then the money can build up over several pre-retirement years. What sort of PEP you choose depends very much on how long you have to go until your projected retirement date – a growth PEP gives you most scope for making money, while an income-generating PEP will help if your needs are more immediate.

3 *Pay off your mortgage*: By this stage in your life you should have plenty of equity in your home. Paying off lump sums or overpaying the mortgage each month should help you reduce the number of years left on your loan. See Chapter 5 for details.

4 *Save*: You should make the most of tax-free opportunities and make sure you and your spouse both have TESSAs.

Boosting income in retirement

MOST OF US WILL FIND that our retirement income isn't enough to meet everyday needs and leave some over. If you need to make some last-minute adjustments in retirement, here are some ideas.

1 *Safe home income plans*: Many pensioners own their homes outright but haven't got any cash. Home income plans are a way to release the value of your home so that you can live off it. These schemes aren't worth considering until you are 70 or more because your age determines how much annual income you'll get from selling a share in your home, or re-mortgaging part of it.

There are two basic types of scheme: a remortgage deal, where you effectively take out a loan for part of the value of your house. The cash sum is then used to buy an annuity, which pays you an income for the rest of your life. That's why you need to be older to make this worthwhile – younger people are offered much lower annuity rates because it's expected that they'll live longer. You don't have to repay this mortgage in your lifetime: the cash will be taken from the money raised by the sale of the house after your death.

The second type of home income scheme is a 'home reversion' scheme, which basically asks you to sell all or part of your house to the home income company. They draw up a deal which allows you to live there for the rest of your life. You can use the cash they give you to buy an annuity.

If you're interested in either type of scheme, get hold of a list of all the companies which are members of the Safe Home Income Plan (SHIP) group, a self-regulating body which guarantees minimum standards in the field. Contact 0181-390 8166 for a list of members.

2 *Income-producing investments*: Corporate bonds PEPs are good news for people who need a regular income. You won't see much capital growth. See Chapter 9.
3 *Check you are getting all the state benefits you're entitled to*: Billions of pounds go unclaimed because people don't realise that they are entitled to benefits in retirement.
4 *Lodgers*: Taking a lodger can produce a good income and it's tax free under the rent-a-room scheme so long as you only earn £81·73 a week or less from the rental. This adds up to £4,250 per year for the 1997/98 tax year.

When your investments aren't working

IF YOU TAKE OUT a PEP, or a unit trust or investment trust savings scheme for a long-term investment and three years' later it's barely worth more than you have put into it, then you may need to revise your investment plans.

Advisers always say that you should be prepared to weather the ups and downs of the stockmarket, but if you feel you made a bad buy then you need to check out your suspicions and sell up if necessary.

It's better to cut your losses and make up the money elsewhere rather than hang on to something that is never going to perform.

Beware of cashing in endowments and friendly society policies because you don't like what you see on your returns in the early years. The charges all go upfront on these deals, so you have to wait a few years before they have a cash-in value, or, in the case of endowments, a value to a buyer on the second-hand market.

First of all you need to make sure you chose the right investment. There's no point in blaming the fund manager if the fund is volatile and risky when you were hoping for a safe and consistent return.

If this isn't the problem, find out what's going on from the fund manager – ask what's being done about the poor performance. Don't switch to a star performer without careful research.

You can switch the investments within a PEP whenever you want. With a self-select PEP it's obviously up to you when you buy and sell the investments held in it. If it's not self-select, don't close the PEP, transfer it to your new manager. Otherwise, you'll lose your PEP allowance for that tax year. Bear in mind you'll incur some dealing costs so be sure the switch will be worthwhile.

Remember to keep an eye on your savings accounts too. One small investor took his building society to court when it failed to pay a competitive rate of interest on its TESSA – as stated in the marketing literature. You may not be able to go as far as that, but remember you can move your money between savings accounts – including TESSAs.

If you have an instant access savings account all you have to do is compare the different rates of interest and choose the best one. If you have a notice account it is usually worthwhile serving out the notice period rather than moving straight away.

If you hadn't realised you could switch your TESSA, check whether it is paying a competitive rate. TESSA providers only have to let you transfer your money out to another TESSA though, they aren't obliged to let you transfer money in. If you want to switch, first work out if a better rate of interest will offset what you may lose through transfer penalties and lost saver incentives. Remember to explain to your existing TESSA provider that you're switching your account, not closing it. If you close it, you'll lose the tax benefits.

You should review your savings and investment plans every one or two years, to ensure things are on track and still suitable.

Action plan

- ❍ Establish what you're saving or investing for and check whether your current savings and investments are really suitable.
- ❍ If you want to build up a nest egg for your children, consider bank and building society accounts, National Savings Children's Bonus Bonds and Premium Bonds.
- ❍ If you want to pay for your children's education and have time to save look at a combination of TESSAs and PEPs.
- ❍ If you hope to retire early, you need to look into boosting your pension contributions and making the most of tax-free savings opportunities.
- ❍ If you're retired and are looking for ways to boost your income, find out if a home income plan would be suitable.
- ❍ If you're worried about the way one of your investments is performing, find out why and don't switch unless the benefits are sure to outweigh any costs.

11 Making a will

"My widowed mother is very elderly and my brother and sister and I do not know what would happen to her house after her death. We think she would like to leave it to my sister and we are all happy with that. Without a will would this be possible? We don't want to broach the subject unless it is absolutely necessary"

This is typical of many letters we get at *Moneywise* magazine – letters that make it very clear why you should make a will. If you don't, it can make things complicated for your heirs, and in some cases may deprive them of something you wanted them to have.

Here are the basic rules on who gets what if you die intestate – without making a will – in England and Wales (we'll deal with Scotland separately). The law in Northern Ireland is almost identical to that in England and Wales. The major exception is that in Northern Ireland people under 18 who are married can make a will. That is not the case in England and Wales. Once you've read the rules, you'll realise that making a will allows you to distribute your wealth among all the people who are dear to you, not just those whom the law says should benefit.

- If you are married without other relatives your husband or wife will inherit the whole estate.
- If you are married without children but have parents, brothers or sisters still alive, your spouse will get the first £200,000 of your estate and half of the rest. The other half goes to your close relatives. A living parent has first claim on all of the money, and then your brothers and sisters, if both your parents are dead.
- If you are married with children, they will be entitled to one half of whatever is left after the first £125,000 has gone to their living parent. Children under 18 must have their money placed in trust until their 18th birthday. If any of your children have died, but you have grandchildren, the money passes directly to them; again, it has to be held in trust if they are under 18. Your spouse will be able to take an income from the other half of what is left, such as money generated by investments, but he or

she can't sell off the assets; they are held in trust and he or she has only a 'life interest'. After the second spouse dies, all the children and/or grandchildren share the capital equally.

- If you have divorced your ex-partner does not get a share of the estate if you die without a will. Any children you've had with an ex-partner have full claims.
- If you live with a partner but you aren't married then the law does not automatically recognise your partner's claim. He or she will have to apply to the Crown administrator for a share of the estate. Any children you've had together have the same full rights whether they are born inside or outside marriage.

> Tax expert and *Moneywise* Ask The Professionals panellist Janet Adam says:
>
> "Even if you don't make a will you can ensure your home passes directly to your spouse or partner by ensuring that you have legal ownership as joint tenants, where your share of the asset automatically passes on death to the surviving owner."

These are just the main ways an estate is split. If you have a complicated family life then it could take years for all the finances to be sorted out and distributed among your relatives. Making a will is especially important if you aren't married – it's one of the areas where the law hasn't caught up with modern lifestyles.

- If you have no living relatives your estate will pass into Crown hands. Anyone who thinks they have a claim on your estate can apply for their share.

You can also use a will to reduce an inheritance tax bill, see Chapter 4 and page 198.

Scotland

Scottish law is very different, especially when it comes to the rules of intestacy. If you die without making a will your spouse gets a right to your house, up to a value of £110,000, its furnishings up to a value of £20,000 and up to £30,000 in cash (or £50,000 if you have no children). The survivor also gets a proportion of everything above this. The children get everything else.

Although it's possible that your children could get nothing if you die intestate in Scotland, you can't cut out your husband or wife, or your children, from your will. And unlike England, a marriage doesn't automatically make any previous will invalid. The tax rules in Scotland are the same as in the rest of the UK.

How to make a will

YOU CAN SAVE MONEY on lawyers' fees by buying a standard form for making a will from a stationers. Don't just write down who should inherit your assets. You need to get the technical jargon right or there'll be plenty of scope for misunderstanding.

A will may be challenged after your death if it's got a paper clip mark on it. It's that petty. (A paperclip might indicate that the will has been changed after you originally wrote it.)

It's best to read up on how to word a will – the Consumers' Association produces a DIY pack called Make Your Own Will. It costs £10.99 and is available by calling 0800 252100.

If you want to write a will and help a good cause, there's a bi-annual charity week in November called Will Aid, when solicitors draw up a will and donate your fee to charity. Check the press for details.

If you have had a complicated personal life – for example, you've got children from two marriages – or you have assets of more than £215,000, which makes you liable for inheritance tax (see Chapter 4), you should see a solicitor and get a will drawn up professionally.

Having a will drawn up isn't expensive (a straightforward will costs about £50 or £75 for couples) and it will put your mind at rest. Find a lawyer through personal recommendation or the local commercial telephone directories but remember to ask about charges before you go ahead.

A firm of professional will-writers will also draw up a will for you, and they tend to be cheaper than a solicitor. The drawback is that some firms are better than others. A will-writer is fine if you have a good personal recommendation and are sure the firm has sufficient knowledge to draw up even a complicated will. Otherwise, play safe and stick with a solicitor. Some banks and life companies also offer will-writing services. Don't bother with these as there's often a hidden 'sting' – the bank may

want you to appoint it as the executor of your will.

Once you've decided who your executors will be – it's a good idea to pick people who are younger than you, and your children can be executors once they are over 18 – then tell them about their role and let them know where they can find a copy of your will. If you've had it drawn up at a solicitor's, you should leave a copy there. Don't just assume your executors will find your will in the safe under the bath – what if no one knows it's there?

How your will is used

The executors read the will at once to find out what your wishes are for your funeral, whether you've made a choice between burial or cremation, for example. Once the immediate arrangements have been made, the executors may need to get probate granted for what you've decided in the will. Probate is a document that gives the executors official permission to collect the money from a dead person's estate and distribute it according to the terms of the will.

How to find out about someone else's will

If you've got an interest in what someone else has said in their will, you can find out as soon as probate has been granted. If you are going to inherit something, the executors should contact you, but you can still contact your local District Probate Registry for a copy of any will. There is a charge for this.

If you're not happy with what you see, remember that a will is not the last word on how an estate is to be distributed. There's plenty of scope for relatives who feel they have a claim to dispute the bequest of all their mother's worldly goods to a dogs' charity, for example. The relatives can say she was unfit to write the will, or under undue influence from someone. Get legal advice if you want to contest a will; you need to start proceedings within six months of probate being granted.

Tax

Making a will is important to ensure that your money goes to those close to you. But you also need to do all you can to reduce or remove any 'death duty' charged to your heirs (or to your estate) after you die.

Inheritance tax (known as IHT) may be due on the estate and on any gifts you've made during the last seven years of your life. Here are some general points to consider before the actual tax planning:

- Although you can leave £215,000 before there is any liability for inheritance tax, the assets easily mount up, especially if there's a house involved. The house will be valued at current market price, so if you bought it back in the 1940s or 1950s you may be shocked to discover how much it's worth.
- There's no tax saving for you personally in all this – in fact, it might cost you money – you will be acting purely for the benefit of your spouse and heirs. And if you aren't careful, you might end up losing control over some of your assets. It's possible you could lose your home, so be very careful, especially if your family do not get on with each other.
- Keep an eye on the Budget every year for changes to inheritance tax that might affect your plans.
- Beware of giving away your home to your children in order to avoid the possibility that you will have to sell up to pay for care in a residential home at the end of your life. Social services departments are aware of what people try to do and you have to act carefully. Changing ownership like this might be classed as 'deliberate deprivation of assets' – giving something away on purpose. You need to take professional advice before you contemplate transferring property.

Most people should have no reason to worry about inheritance tax. The vast majority of estates don't add up to more than £215,000. Even if you have a reasonably large estate, everything you leave to your husband or to your wife is exempt from tax. Some other bequests are tax free as well, including gifts to charities. But if you don't do any planning and leave everything to your spouse, your heirs may get hit with a big IHT bill. Everything you leave over the

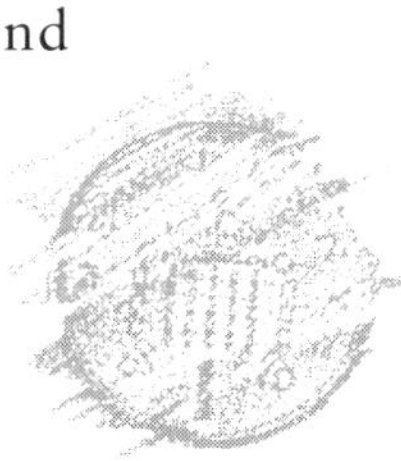

£215,000 mark will be taxed at the higher, 40% tax rate.

There is a way round this – with professional help, your spouse can reduce the tax bill by transferring some of your assets in the two years after your death as if you were still alive. However, this route is very complicated and, in any case, should be unnecessary if you make careful plans which will reduce the overall value of your estate before you die. Basically, this means giving your money away!

> Tax expert and *Moneywise* Ask The Professionals panellist Janet Adam says:
>
> "It is always a good idea to keep some form of written record of gifts you have made. A list will do but, ideally, a copy of a letter sent with every gift provides contemporary evidence both of the amount and date of the gift. This is especially important for large gifts."

Give some tax-free gifts

All these ways to make gifts will allow you to pass on some of your assets: there is no inheritance tax to pay after your death either for your estate or for the person who received the gift. If you are giving away items such as jewellery and shares, you won't always be liable for capital gains tax when you transfer ownership to someone else and the person who receives the gift won't be liable for any capital gains tax until they sell them (see below).Even then they can use up their tax exemption (worth £6,500 in the 1997/98 tax year). Always keep records of what you have transferred to whom, and how much each item was worth (both when you bought it originally, and an estimated current value in the case of jewellery and other valuables). This should make sorting out your estate easier.

- You can give away a total of £3,000-worth of gifts in any tax year. If you didn't use any of your allowance the previous year, then you'll have £6,000 to give away in 1997/98. There are several other ways in which you can give away money and valuables (see below) so that they don't fall within this £3,000 allowance.
- You can make as many small tax-free gifts during your lifetime as you like. Anything worth £250 or less counts as a tax-free gift, but beware – once the value rises above £251 you have to set this against your main tax-free gift allowance.

- Regular payments made out of your after-tax income can be made tax-free. A good way to make use of this rule is to take out an insurance policy or convert an existing one so that you pay the premiums but hold the policy in trust for someone else, who will be paid when it matures, or when you die (if it's a life policy).
- When a child or grandchild gets married you can make a one-off tax-free gift. If you're a parent you can offer £5,000 and a grandparent or great-grandparent can give £2,500. Anyone else can give £1,000 to newly-weds.
- If you want to leave some money in your will to a favourite charity, or give a donation to a museum or art gallery, then you could offer the money before you die, tax-free. This has the advantage that you may be able to see what they've done with the money. All gifts to charities – and political parties – are exempt from tax, however much you give.

MAKE SOME POTENTIALLY TAX-FREE GIFTS

Another set of rules covers gifts which don't fall into any of the tax-exempt categories. You might potentially be liable for inheritance tax, if you make a gift, if your estate is worth more than £215,000 and you die within seven years of giving the gift. There is a sliding tax scale, so that the recipient would only have to pay 20% of the total tax due on the gift if you died in the seventh year after handing it over. The tax is calculated on the value of the gift at the time that you passed it on to the new owner. This sort of gift is referred to as a 'potentially exempt transfer' or PET.

SET UP A TRUST

If you've got a large or complicated estate you may want to set up a trust to protect your assets. By putting the assets into a trust, you fence them off from the rest of your estate. These arrangements allow a range of assets, such as your house, to be placed within the trust. The income or proceeds from a sale is distributed among named beneficiaries, for example, your grandchildren. Trust law is complex and you need to consult a lawyer to make sure this is the right step

and that the benefits will definitely outweigh the costs. The most common type of trusts used by people who are passing on their assets are:

Example

You and your spouse have assets worth £600,000 divided equally between you. If one spouse dies leaving the other his or her £300,000, there is no IHT because gifts to spouses are exempt.

But when the other spouse dies and leaves the whole £600,000 to the family, IHT will be payable on £385,000 (£600,000 less the £215,000 nil rate band). So, at 40% the tax bill would be £154,000. You need a clause in each will establishing a trust. The amount of the nil rate band, £215,000, goes into the trust.

When the second spouse dies and the whole estate is left to the family, IHT of £68,000 will be payable on £170,000 – the second spouse's estate of £385,000 less his or her nil rate band.

- *Discretionary trusts*: These allow you to name all the people whom you want to benefit from your estate. You can control the income and capital that they receive while you're still alive. The drawback is, however, that you may be liable to pay tax if you put more than £215,000 into a discretionary trust – at the time when you pay it in. Tax has to be paid on any amount above the IHT threshold. It doesn't necessarily have to be paid in one lump – if the value of the transfers into the trust goes over £215,000 (or the current IHT limit), paid in during any seven-year period, then that triggers a tax charge. This charge is paid at 20% – half of the IHT rate. If you die within seven years of putting the money in trust, then additional tax (up to the normal 40% charge) may be incurred under the PET rules (see details above). Your heirs may have to pay tax on the income from the trust, depending on their own tax position, but this will generally be cheaper than allowing the estate to be taxed under normal conditions.
- *Accumulation and maintenance trusts*: These are trusts which are set up to pay for children's and grandchildren's education. The income from the trust is taxed but this can be claimed back if the children benefiting from the trust aren't taxpayers. If you die within seven years of putting the money into the trust, then inheritance tax may have to be paid on a sliding scale. Children who benefit from this sort of trust have to receive the income they are entitled to before they are 25, although you could state that the capital should be left in trust, for example, until they are 35.

Action plan

- If you haven't made a will, you should to ensure that your survivors get what you want them to have.
- If you're prepared to spend time rather than money, look into using a DIY pack.
- If your circumstances are quite complicated, it's better to get a solicitor to draw up your will for you.
- If you are concerned about inheritance tax, which has to be paid on your estate if it's worth more than £215,000, ensure your will takes advantage of the rules which keep the bill down.

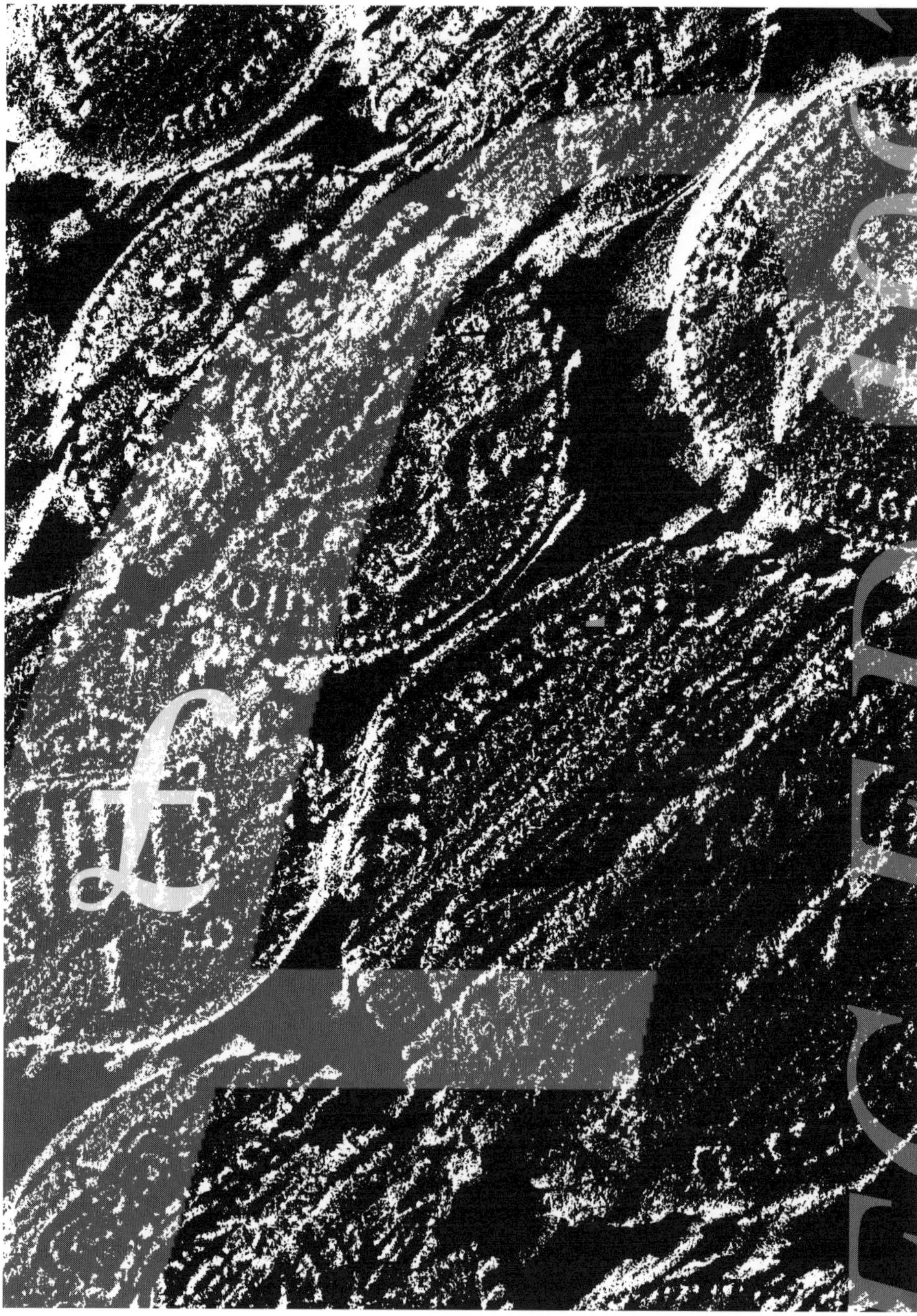

12
Getting advice

***Moneywise* asked an investment manager who deals with financial advisers every day, to give readers some tips on how to find a good adviser. "It's like finding a good plumber. The best idea is to get a personal recommendation from someone you trust. If you can't get that you can always find one in the *Yellow Pages*. They might be great or they might be terrible." In other words, it's a lottery. And although financial advisers won't like being compared with plumbers, the fact is that the industry is diverse – to say the least.**

Sadly, there are some third-rate advisers out there, whether they're independent or are just working for one company. You may not be aware that there are two types of financial adviser: those who work for one firm only and those who are independent. Be aware that the nice adviser at the bank is only selling you the bank's own products.

You may be suspicious of the 'independent' status of an adviser who is paid through commission – an adviser is hardly going to recommend a product which pays little or no commission over one which comes with a hefty payoff. There is no such thing as free advice. Someone has to pay for the advice you're getting, and for the marketing and running costs of whatever products you end up buying. If you pop in to the bank or see the man from the Pru, it's the same. The commission isn't always obvious – Equitable Life, for example, says it pays no commission to middlemen and women. That's true – Equitable doesn't pay IFAs who recommend its products, but it pays its own salespeople a very good salary and, of course, they can recommend only Equitable's own products.

In this chapter we'll look at the different sources of financial advice and how you can work the system to your advantage. There's nothing to stop you using several advisers and playing them off against each other. And then there's DIY financial planning – which should be easy once you've read this book.

Financial advisers

COMPANY SALESPEOPLE

How do I recognise a salesperson who only works for one company? These advisers are known in the finance trade as 'tied' salespeople because they are tied to one firm. The adviser who sees you in the bank is just as much a tied salesperson as the life insurance rep who cold-calls you at work. (In finance jargon, you're a 'name' or a 'prospect' to these people. They buy lists of 'names' likely to generate business.)

All banks and building societies, with the exception of the Co-operative Bank and the Bradford & Bingley, have branch-based advisers who only sell the company's own products.

A salesperson who works for one of the big life companies, such as Prudential or Equitable Life, can sell you only that company's products.

How to use them to your advantage: You can get a free financial planning makeover from your bank, building society or a tied rep who visits you at home. These advisers are obliged to get a full picture of your current finances and your planning needs before they attempt to sell you anything. If you have been following the advice in this book but would like some more help, or are looking for new ideas, then go ahead and get them to do some work on your behalf.

What to avoid: Buying what they recommend. They can only sell you their own company's products. Go away and compare what the tied salesperson has said with your own research. You could also visit an independent adviser for a more complete picture of what's available and what your priorities should be (see below).

If you can't be bothered with hassle and feel that you'd be happy to buy something the tied adviser recommends, then go ahead. It won't be unsuitable as a general investment or protection scheme – but it's unlikely to be the best policy of its type on the market.

How to find a good tied adviser: If you understand that you won't get impartial advice or be offered the best product for your needs, but you still want to stay with one company, you should pick one with a good track record. That can be hard to find out – all firms present information selectively to show themselves in a good light. You can check general performance in *Money*

Management magazine, aimed at finance professionals, which costs £4·95 from newsagents. It carries regular surveys on different financial products and publishes performance tables for stockmarket investments every month. Ask your adviser if he or she is salaried, works for commission only, or a basic wage plus commission. That will give you an idea of how much pressure he or she is under to sell to every client.

Independent financial advisers

What does independent mean, anyway? That's the $6 million question. The idea is that an independent adviser takes a good look at your current financial position, tells you what action you should take, and suggests the best products on the market. They can recommend any products and most of them give the advice for free. They are paid by commission as a 'thank you' from the company which sells you the 'winning' products.

The classy end of the IFA business charges an hourly fee to clients, like solicitors and accountants. Some of these fee-charging advisers are practising solicitors and accountants who are qualified to give financial advice. Expect to pay up to £150 an hour for a highly qualified IFA or accountant or solicitor who gives advice. You should get commission payments rebated to you if you pay a fee.

IFAs who are paid by commission protest that it doesn't influence them. However, some finance companies don't pay commission (including telephone-based firms like Virgin Direct and the banks' and building societies' financial arms, known as *bancassurers*) because they sell enough to customers without needing IFA business. An IFA will tell you that non-commission paying firms don't offer the best deals on the market. If you pay a fee, you do at least get peace of mind that commission isn't playing a part in all this.

How to use them to your advantage: IFAs have to offer you a comprehensive financial questionnaire before they can make any recommendations about what you should do next. The results should be useful, whether or not you go on to buy products from the adviser.

Most IFAs specialise in a particular area. Find out what their strengths are and whether they match your objectives. For example, you may be happy to plan your own insurance and protection but want some help in selecting stockmarket investments. An IFA who calls him or herself an investment adviser should be able to give you long-term help in this area.

Ask about payment on your first visit – a lot of firms will be very straightforward about this. If money isn't mentioned, avoid the firm. Don't be afraid that you'll be asked to pay cash on the first visit. The vast majority of IFAs are paid by commission only. If you don't buy anything, you won't pay anything!

What to avoid: Some firms of IFAs don't really operate a totally independent service. They have a 'panel' of a few favoured firms whose products they offer first to clients. It's likely that experience has shown that these firms offer good deals to most people – but they might not suit your needs. Ask the IFA if the firm operates from a panel or is totally independent.

Most IFAs are fully computerised and hooked up to big information databases giving the latest premiums for insurance policies and performance statistics for investments. If the firm doesn't have up-to-date technology, you should look elsewhere.

Finding a competent adviser

It's no wonder that financial advice has a bad name. Until July 1997 advisers could be employed with no qualifications at all. There was a massive turnover within sales teams. The mis-selling of personal pensions to people who should have stayed in safe employers schemes seems to have been an inevitable side-effect of giving salespeople no training while offering big commission payments for pension sales.

In a bid to clean up the industry and make it more professional, minimum qualifications are now in place. This is what you should look for after an adviser's name.

The bare minimum

Tied and independent advisers had to pass three exams by 1 July 1997. Several bodies run exams that are accepted qualifications:

- The one you'll see most often is the FPC (Financial Planning Certificate) run by the Chartered Insurance Institute. Most financial advisers take these exams, so they should have passed FPC 1, 2 and 3.

- The Certificate for Financial Advisers (CeFA) run by the Chartered Institute of Bankers (CIB). Parts 1, 2 and 3.
- The Investment Advice Certificate (IAC) from the Securities Institute. Parts 1, 2 and 3.
- Advisers who are aged 55 and who have been working in the business for ten years or more only have to pass papers 1 and 2 of any of these exams. They can take an oral test instead of the (hardest) paper 3.

How to find a qualified adviser
Call IFA Promotion on 01171 971 1177. This organisation will send you the names and contact numbers for four independent advice firms near your home or work. There's no extra information supplied so you'll have to do your own research to find out more about each firm.

ADVANCED QUALIFICATIONS

If you are looking for help with complex investments and tax planning, go to a solicitor or accountant who also offers financial advice, or a financial adviser with a professional qualification.

Financial advisers who want a higher qualification than the above can choose between the Advanced Financial Planning Certificate from the CII or the Professional Investment Certificate from the CIB and the Institute of Financial Planning. There is also the internationally recognised Certified Financial Planner certificate (CFP), which is only available from the Institute of Financial Planning (see below). Advisers applying for the CFP must have passed the AFPC or the Institute of Financial Planning's own Fellowship exam. Anyone who gets the CFP has to follow strict educational and ethical rules and renew their application every year. *How to find a qualified adviser*: IFAs and accountants with advanced qualifications may be members (either Associate or Fellows) of the Institute of Financial Planning. The IFP has an information pack giving full details of member firms which charge fees to clients. Call 0171 930 4434.

Chartered accountants must have passed the Initial Test of Competence (ITC); an accountant can take any of the recognised sets of exams above. Firms, not individuals, are registered to carry out investment business. You can get a list of local registered firms through the Practitioner Bureau (01171 920 8682) or look for your local District Society of Chartered Accountants in the *Yellow Pages*.

Solicitors have to be certified to carry out investment business. The Law Society regulates 7,200 firms which also give financial advice. Some firms have partners who are qualified investment advisers and others employ financial planners to work alongside solicitors. The Association of Solicitor Investment Managers (ASIM) has a free directory of firms which offer financial planning as a main part of their business. Call 01892 870065. Or there's the Solicitors for Financial Advice (SIFA) network, which has a hotline number: 01372 721172.

> Independent financial adviser and *Moneywise* Ask the Professionals panellist Brian Dennehy says:
>
> "Sorting out your paperwork before the meeting will ensure you're not wasting both your the time and the IFA's. Perhaps more importantly it should help you focus on your precise objectives and what financial arrangements you've already made before you see the IFA. Your objectives should lead where the meeting goes – why not send details through ahead of the meeting?"

MEETING A FINANCIAL ADVISER

1 Once you have picked a firm you like the look of, make an initial appointment. The adviser needs to find out as much as possible about you, your family, and your plans for the future. Take as many financial documents as you can to the meeting – your endowment policy, statement of pension contributions, mortgage payments, and so on. If you have sickness benefits provided through your employers, such as private medical insurance or an income replacement scheme, then take along the details. The more information the adviser has, the more he or she will be able to help you.

2 The adviser has to introduce the firm, so you should be given what's known as a 'terms of business' letter. This sets out whether you're seeing an independent or tied adviser. A good firm should also let you know how the adviser earns his or her money. In a reputable IFA firm, that's likely to be from a salary plus commission on products sold. Many firms offer the option of paying by fees (see above) but most clients don't want this. Look for an adviser with an open approach, who gives you lots of information.

3 During the first meeting the adviser will carry out what's known as a 'fact find' about you, based on your discussion and all the information you've brought with you. This is usually written

up on a standard questionnaire and will form the basis for any recommendations the adviser makes. After the meeting you should get a written report, outlining what the adviser suggests should be your priorities and giving product recommendations. Some firms prefer to discuss findings in a second face-to-face meeting, while others are happy for you to digest the findings and then chat over the phone. If you feel you are being given the hard sell, don't feel obliged to buy anything. A good adviser won't expect you to act on the report straightaway. They want your long-term business.

4 There's nothing to stop you taking up recommendations by buying direct from the product provider. But bear in mind that it's a myth that you'll get a cheaper deal on most products by going direct. There's a marketing cost built into personal pensions, for example, and if you go direct the company simply keeps that money or gives a small incentive to their telephone operators, rather than paying full commission to the independent salesperson who sold you the pension (that's why firms are so keen to sell pensions direct to the public). For example, an endowment policy pays a lot of commission to the person who sold it to you. You'll notice that most endowments have very low cash-in values for the first few years after they have been out – that's because a large slice of your early payments goes on commission to advisers and the setting-up costs of the plan.

If you look as though you know what you're talking about, you can negotiate a discount from your adviser, asking him or her to offer you part of the commission as cash or paid back into your investment. If you can't get the adviser to cut the commission on PEPs, save yourself money by going to an execution-only PEP sales firm (see the section on DIY financial planning, below). These firms operate on very tight margins. They rebate most or all of the initial charge – which is up to 5% of any investment up to £6,000. (The commission normally paid to the adviser is taken from this charge.) PEP sales firms stay in business by keeping an annual commission paid by the fund manager if you renew your business every year.

You don't have to pay 'extra' money to cover commission payments. Commission is built into the charges you have to pay on everything you buy.

5 A little-known bonus of using an independent financial adviser is that any claim you have to make on a health policy, for example, will be dealt with through the IFA's office. So if you become very ill and have an income replacement policy bought from an IFA, you'll be able to claim via your adviser. At a time when you and your family are bound to be under a lot of strain, you can leave sorting out the money to someone who isn't directly involved. An IFA will be able to get through to the right people on your behalf – and should get you a swift result. Buying any investment or insurance policy through an adviser's recommendation gives you financial protection if something goes very wrong, you were badly advised, or the firm goes bust and you lose money.

Investment management

LOTS OF STOCKBROKERS and investment managers offer a portfolio management service to people who have lots of money to invest and aren't interested in running their own finances.

Typically, you need £25,000 or more before a firm will take you on as a private client. Stockbrokers will put your money into a basket of shares, and it's likely they'll pick individual shares they consider to be a good investment bet, rather than spreading your cash among collective funds such as OEICS, unit trusts and investment trusts. These investments reduce the risk to your money by pooling investors' money and buying lots of shares in different companies (see page 163).

The charges on privately managed portfolios tend to be high – there's a charge every time your broker buys and sells shares, plus you may be liable for capital gains tax when you sell. Alternatively, look at a managed portfolio service from an accountant, solicitor or independent adviser who specialises in investment business (see 'Advanced qualifications' on page 209).

Many of the banks and investment managers also have a balanced portfolio scheme for people with £50,000 or more. Typically, they'll offer you a growth or income option and your money will be spread among the firm's own collective funds that managers think will perform well. The snag here is the 'one size fits all' approach and the fact that your money is stuck in one firm's funds. A better alternative for conservative investors may be an independent fund of funds investment. Your money is invested in unit trusts, selected across the whole market, which the fund of fund managers believe will do well. See page 163 for more details of this.

DIY financial planning

If you've read this book you'll have a pretty good idea of how to work out your own financial planning needs and how to get the best buys in each area. But you really have nothing to lose by going to see a good financial adviser for an initial review of your finances. If you don't want to act on the recommendations, there's nothing to pay in terms of commission or fees unless you have an arrangement to pay by the hour.

If you have a complex financial life and want some advice on tax and estate planning, for example, you should see an accountant or solicitor who also gives investment advice, to combine both professional functions in one service. Be prepared to pay by the hour. It could save you thousands in the long term. Having said that, here are some ways to get the most from doing your own financial planning:

1 *Do your research*: You need to enjoy this because you'll end up spending lots of time finding out about different savings and investment opportunities. Start by reading the weekend financial press and magazines like *Moneywise*. You'll be amazed how much you can pick up very quickly. File interesting features for future reference. Make use of free offers of information booklets produced by finance companies. Of course they want your name for their marketing database, but many of these guides are well-written and useful.

2 *Ask the right questions*: Before you put money into any investment make sure you understand exactly what you are buying:

- *Is this right for my needs?* There's no point locking yourself into a five-year guaranteed bond investment, for example, if there's a chance you might need that money before the end of the term.

- *Do I understand the small print?* Make sure you know what you are buying. We often get letters from people whose endowment plan hasn't paid out on maturity. What they've been sold is a term assurance plan with no maturity payout.
- *Is this the best deal I'm going to get?* The insurance market is very competitive and for your own sake you should make the most of it. Don't just automatically accept a renewal quote from your existing insurer. Phone four or five direct operators, who will have access to policies across the market, and speak to a broker. There are some brokers who operate over the telephone in the same way as direct insurers.

  If you know which PEP you want, don't just buy it from the investment firm. Go through one of the discount brokers which advertise in the weekend press. They reduce or remove the initial charge you have to pay for taking out the PEP. A typical initial charge is 3%, so on a full £6,000 PEP investment you'd save £180, which would be rebated into your PEP account. Remember that you haven't got any rights to complain if you buy a PEP without taking advice first.

3 *Keep an eye on your investments*: It's easy enough to put some money into a savings account and to forget about it. The majority of us don't know what rate of interest we're getting, and banks and building societies have a habit of opening flash new accounts and allowing older accounts to languish, paying lower rates of interest. They only have to tell you once a year if there's been a rate change.

   Keep an eye on your savings, checking the interest rates posted in the local branch or by phoning up every few months. Watch out for new accounts, which will be launched with a fanfare of press advertisements. Find out if these are open to existing investors? If you're with a building society, will you still be able to claim membership rights if you move your money?

   Unit and investment trust prices are printed in the broadsheet papers. You can check them every day if you want, although once a month is probably the best bet. Note down what each unit is worth every month, so you have an idea of how your investments are going. If they are consistently poor performers, you should think about swapping them for something with a decent track record.

Independent financial adviser and *Moneywise* Ask the Professionals panellist Brian Dennehy says:

"Every fund has a bad patch. But it's important you weed out as early as possible those funds which are consistently poor relative to their peers, and those which on reflection don't match your original objectives."

4 *Hang on to every bit of paper*: Keep your investment correspondence in different files in case there's a problem. The new tax rules mean you'll need to keep track of investments and dividends paid. Remember, you aren't as well protected if something goes wrong as if you'd made your plans through a financial adviser.

If things go wrong

The complaints and compensation system for the financial services industry is a byzantine mess – that's why Chancellor Gordon Brown made reforming the system a priority when Labour came to power in May 1997.

Here's an outline of what to do at the moment if you have a problem and want to sort things out.

1 *Decide what sort of redress you're looking for*: Would you be happy with an apology for poor service or rudeness, or are you looking for compensation? Be clear from the outset, and make it clear in all your correspondence on the subject.
2 *Complain locally first*: In most cases the best idea is to approach the problem informally, and try to sort it out at a local level. That means going to the salesperson or firm which gave you financial advice, the bank branch you feel unhappy with, or the unit trust management firm which has bodged the sale of your holdings. Put your concerns in writing, with back-up evidence if needed. It's vital for later stages of the current complaints process that you know who sold you a product or policy which is causing a problem.
3 *If you're not happy with the response you get*: If this happens, then you should ask a bank or building society, for example, to deal with it through its formal complaints procedure. For other firms you should ring the head office and ask for the name of the managing director. Always write to people by name.

4 *Check that you are entitled to help*: Be warned – some investments are not covered by laws which protect investors. Basically, if you buy something tangible, which you can examine, such as an ostrich, whisky, antiques or gemstones, then you aren't entitled to compensation if something goes wrong. Be very wary of schemes which sound too good to be true. They are often set up to make the founders rich at the expense of naive investors. If you're not sure whether you're protected under consumer law, call the Securities & Investments Board (SIB). This organisation has a register of all the businesses which are approved to carry out investment business and will be able to tell you if an investment is covered by financial protection laws. You can call this Central Register on 0171 929 3652 to check.
5 *If the business which advised you has gone bust*: If there's no one to deal with your complaint, you can still get compensation. The Investors Compensation Scheme was set up to help people like you. It is funded by the finance industry. Get in touch with the ICS at the same address as SIB, above. Telephone 0171 628 8820.
6 *Go along to the regulator*: All financial advisers, investment managers and stockbrokers are regulated by organisations set up to make sure they follow the rules. The first step is to work out which of the regulators are responsible for supervising the firm which sold you the product. You may have some company notepaper which states which body regulates the firm, which will point you in the right direction. Public libraries and Citizens' Advice Bureaux also give help.
7 *Take the case to an independent assessor*: If you aren't happy with the way the company and the regulator has handled your complaint, then you can go to the relevant ombudsman's office. The ombudsmen investigate problems and can demand redress if they find in your favour. This can take various forms – not all of them have the right to demand cash payments from firms which are found to be at fault:
   - If you have a problem with a bank or building society, then there are two places that can help. If you're complaining about a savings account or mortgage advice go to the Banking (0171 404 9944)or Building Society Ombudsman (0171 931 0044). If you bought an investment such as a

PEP or a personal pension from a bank or building society, or from any tied or independent financial adviser, call the Personal Investment Authority (PIA) Ombudsman (0171 216 0016)

- Questions about employers pensions should go to OPAS, the Occupational Pensions Advisory Service (0171 233 8080).
- Anything you have bought direct from an investment house, such as a unit trust or investment trust, will probably be regulated by the Investment Ombudsman, whose job is to mediate in disputes concerning members of the Investment Management Regulatory Organisation (IMRO) (0171 796 3065).
- There is a Legal Services Ombudsman if you aren't happy with your treatment from the self-regulating body representing solicitors (0161 236 9532).
- You can still go to court if you are unhappy with the way you have been treated by the complaints body. The only exception to this is for complaints against stockbrokers, whose professional body, the Securities & Futures Authority (SFA) runs an independent arbitration service (0171 378 9000). If you take part in the service you have to abide by its decision. There is no Ombudsman service.

Action plan

- To find a good adviser, try and get a recommendation – but make sure the adviser is authorised by calling the SIB Central Register on 0171 929 3652,
- Take advantage of as much free advice as you can.
- Decide what you're prepared to spend for financial advice – if you're happy to pay a fee, look for a fee-based IFA.
- It makes sense to approach a few advisers to ensure you find someone you're happy with.
- Find out what qualifications the advisers you approach have to ensure they are competent.
- Use the information in this book to make sure you're as clued up as possible on financial planning before you see an adviser.

An A–Z guide to financial words and phrases

Accrual rate The rate at which pension entitlement builds up. Often expressed as a fraction of your final salary for each year served, for example 1/60, 1/80. Can be used to refer to Inland Revenue limits on how a pension entitlement builds up. Also can refer to the actual pension entitlement built up for each year of membership of a final salary company pension scheme.
Additional voluntary contributions (AVCs) Extra payments paid into company pension schemes by members to improve their benefits.
Annual percentage rate (APR) The real cost, in terms of interest and fees, of credit (used for comparison purposes).
Annuity A form of income bought through insurance companies with the proceeds from a pension fund, which pays a guaranteed sum throughout your lifetime.
Base rate The interest rate set by the Bank of England, used as a basis for the rates that banks offer their customers.
Basic state pension Flat rate pension payable to all individuals who have made sufficient National Insurance contributions.
Bid-to-offer spread The difference between the price at which investments can be bought and the price at which they can then be sold.
Bond A certificate of debt issued by companies and governments to raise cash, usually paying interest and traded in a market.
Capital gains tax (CGT) The tax payable on profits from the sale of assets, particularly shares.
Contracting out A legal arrangement under which you can give up part of your SERPS benefits and build up an equivalent or better benefit in a company scheme or personal pension.
Convertible A security, usually a bond or debenture issued by a company, that can be converted into the ordinary shares or preference shares of that company at a fixed date or dates, and at a fixed price.
Deed of covenant A promise made in a deed, often used as a means of providing funds to charities or to transfer income from one person to another, with a view to saving tax.
Derivative A financial instrument that is valued according to the expected price movements of an underlying asset, for example a share or a currency.
Dividend The distribution of part of the earnings of a company to its shareholders
Earnings per share (EPS) The earnings of a company over a stated period, usually a year, divided by the number of ordinary shares it has issued.
Endowment policy A life insurance and savings policy which pays a specified amount of money on an agreed date, or on the death of the person insured, whichever is sooner.
Equities The ordinary shares of a publicly quoted company.
European Currency Unit (ECU) A form of currency calculated as a weighted average of a basket of EC currencies.
Final salary pension scheme a Company pension scheme in which your pension depends on your salary at retirement, your number of years' service, and the fraction of final salary awarded for each year's service, for example 1/60.

Free-standing additional voluntary contributions (FSAVCs) Extra payments made to boost a pension by investing with an insurance company, not an employers scheme. See 'AVCs'.
Friendly Society A mutual organisation offering tax-free investment plans with a life-insurance element, normally over ten years.
Fund A reserve of money or investments held for a specific purpose – for example, to be divided into units for investors to buy (as in a unit trust fund) or to provide a pension income (as in a pension fund).
Future A contract to buy or sell a fixed number of commodities, currencies, or shares at a fixed date in the future at a fixed price.
Gearing The ratio of the amount of long-term loans and preference shares to ordinary shares in a company.
Gilt-edged security (gilt) A fixed-interest security issued by the British Government.
Guaranteed income bond (GIB) A bond guaranteeing the full return of capital plus a fixed income, issued by life insurance companies.
Held in trust An arrangement allowing property or cash to be held by a trustee on behalf of a named beneficiary.
Independent financial adviser (IFA) An adviser committed to offering 'best advice' on the range of investments and plans in the marketplace, not someone selling investments from just one company.
Inheritance tax (IHT) A form of wealth tax on inherited money: £215,000 can be inherited before this tax is incurred.
Initial charge The charge paid to the managers of a unit trust by an investor when he or she first buys units – usually between 3% and 5%.
Investment trust A company quoted on the stock exchange which invests in other companies' shares.
Lower earnings limit (LEL) Weekly wage roughly equivalent to the basic state pension. If you earn less than this amount, you do not pay National Insurance contributions. If you earn more that the LEL, your earnings up to the upper earnings limit (UEL) are liable to National Insurance contributions. Earnings between the LEL and the UEL are called middle band earnings.
Middle band earnings Earnings between the lower and upper earnings limits. The SERPS pension relates to these earnings.
Money purchase pension scheme A company pension scheme in which your pension is dependent on the amount paid into the pension fund, and the investment performance of that fund.
Mortgage interest relief at source (MIRAS) Tax relief at 15% (10% from April 1998) on the interest on the first £30,000 borrowed to buy a house.
National Insurance contributions Contributions payable on earnings if you earn more than the lower earnings limit, to pay for state benefits and pensions.
Negative equity The condition whereby the current market value of a house is worth less than the amount outstanding on a mortgage.
Net relevant earnings Earnings from self-employment or employment which are used to calculate the maximum payments into a personal pension.
Nominees Individuals or companies which hold shares on behalf of investors, to reduce the costs of administering a portfolio, or to conceal the true owners of the shares.
Offshore funds Funds based outside the UK for tax reasons.
Open market option The right to use a pension fund on retirement to buy an annuity from any insurance company, not just the provider of the pension plan.
Option A contract giving the right (but not the obligation) to buy or sell commodities, currencies or shares at a fixed date in the future at a fixed price.
Pay as you earn (PAYE) The system whereby employers collect tax from employees and pass it on to the Inland Revenue.
Penny shares Securities with a very low market price – investors usually hope for rapid recoveries or takeovers.
Pensionable earnings Earnings on which pension benefits and/or contributions are calculated.

Pensionable service The length of time in a particular job which qualifies for pension benefit. Usually this equates to the length of time as a member of the pension scheme.
Pension transfer A payment made from one pension scheme to another, or to an insurance company running a personal pension scheme to fund a buy-out scheme. Enables pension rights to be moved out of the pension scheme of a previous employer.
Permanent health insurance (PHI) Insurance which replaces income lost due to long-term illness or injury and pays benefits relative to the size of a salary.
Personal allowances Amounts of income which you are allowed tax free.
Personal equity plan (PEP) A plan used to hold UK shares, unit trusts, investment trusts, and now corporate bonds, with any dividends and capital gains free of tax.
Personal pension plan An approved scheme for people who are self-employed or not in a company scheme. Personal pensions are arranged through insurance companies, and are individual money purchase schemes.
Preserved pensions Pension rights built up in a pension scheme, which have been left in that scheme when you ceased employment with that company.
Price/earnings ratio (P/E ratio) The market price of a company share divided by the earnings per share of that company.
Retail price index (RPI) The official measure of inflation calculated by weighting the costs of goods and services to approximate a typical family spending pattern.
Retirement annuity contract A type of personal pension superseded in 1988 by personal pensions themselves.
Rights issue New shares sold by a company to raise new capital.
Scrip issue The issue of new share certificates to existing shareholders to reflect an accumulation of profits on the balance sheet.
Self-invested personal pension (SIPP) A personal pension under which the member has the ability to control the investments.
Share An investment in and part ownership of a company, conferring the right to part of the company's profits (usually by payment of a dividend), and to any voting rights attached to that share, and which, in the case of public companies, can be traded on the open market.
Split-capital investment trust A limited-life investment trust in which the equity capital is divided into income shares and capital shares.
State earnings-related pension scheme (SERPS) A state pension in addition to the basic state pension, plus widows' benefits and invalidity benefits, based on earnings.
Stockmarket A market for the buying and selling of shares and securities.
Tax-exempt special savings accounts (TESSAs) Five-year savings accounts which are exempt from tax, and available from banks and building societies.
Tax year The tax system works on the basis of tax years which run from 6 April one calendar year to 5 April the next.
Term assurance or insurance Life insurance with no investment element.
Unit-linked policy An insurance policy in which the benefits depend on the performance of units in a fund invested in shares or property.
Unit trust A pooled fund of stockmarket investments divided into equal units.
Upper earnings limit The maximum weekly wage above which there is no liability to National Insurance contributions.
Value-added tax (VAT) A form of indirect taxation borne by traders and consumers, levied on goods and services.
Whole-of-life policy A life insurance policy which pays a specified amount on the death of the life insured.
With-profits policy A life insurance or pension policy with additional amounts added to the sum insured.
Yield The income from an investment.
Zero-rated Goods or services that are liable to VAT, but with a tax rate of zero.

Directory

REGULATORY BODIES

Investment Managers Regulatory Organisation (IMRO)
Lloyds Chambers, 1 Portsoken Street, London E1 8BT
0171 390 5000

Investors' Compensation Scheme (ICS)
Gavrelle House, 2–14 Bunhill Row, London EC1Y 8RA
0171 638 1240

The Office of the Investment Ombudsman
6 Frederick's Place,
London EC2R 8BT
0171 769 3065

Personal Investment Authority (PIA)
1 Canada Square, Canary Wharf, London E14 5AZ
0171 538 8860

Securities and Futures Authority Ltd (SFA)
Cotton Centre, Cottons Lane, London SE1 2QB
0171 378 9000

Securities and Investments Board (SIB)
Gavrelle House, 2–14 Bunhill Row, London EC1Y 8RA
0171 638 1240
SIB Central Register (address as above) 0171 929 3652

SAVINGS AND INVESTMENTS

Association of Investment Trust Companies (AITC)
Durrant House, 8–13 Chiswell Street, London EC1Y 4YY
0171 588 5347

Association of Policy Market Makers
Holywell Centre, 1 Phipp Street, London EC2A 4PS
0171 739 3949
(for a list of companies selling second-hand endowments)

Association of Solicitor Investment Managers (ASIM)
Baldocks, Chiddingstone Causeway, Tonbridge, Kent TN11 8JX
01892 870065

Association of Private Client Investment Managers
112 Middlesex Street,
London E1 7HY.
0171 247 7080

Association of Unit Trusts and Investment Funds (AUTIF)
Information Unit, 65 Kingsway, London WC2B 6TD
0171 831 0898

National Savings Information
Room 073, Charles House,
376 Kensington High Street,
London W14 8SD
0645 645000

ProShare
Library Chambers,
13–14 Basinghall Street,
London EC2V 5BQ
0171 600 0984

Stock Exchange
Old Broad Street,
London EC2N 1HP
0171 588 2355

BANKS AND BUILDING SOCIETIES

British Bankers' Association
105–108 Old Broad Street
London EC2N 1EX
0171 216 8800

Banking Ombudsman
70 Grays Inn Road,
London WC1X 8NB
0171 404 9944

Building Societies Association/Council of Mortgage Lenders
3 Savile Row, London W1X 1AF
0171 437 0655

Building Societies Ombudsman
Millbank Tower, Millbank,
London SW1P 4XS
0171 931 0044

PENSIONS

Association of Consulting Actuaries (ACA)
1 Wardrobe Place,
London EC4V 5AH
0171 248 3163

Occupational Pensions Advisory Service
11 Belgrave Road,
London SW1V 1RB
0171 233 8080

Pensions Ombudsman
11 Belgrave Road,
London SW1V 1RB
0171 834 9144

CREDIT REFERENCE AGENCIES

CCN Group Ltd
Consumer Help Service,
PO Box 40,
Nottingham NG7 2SS
0115 986 8172

Equifax Europe Ltd
Consumer Affairs Department,
Spectrum House, 1A North Avenue, Clydebank,
Glasgow G81 2DR
0141 951 1253

FINANCIAL ADVICE

Independent Financial Advice Promotion (IFAP)
4th Floor, 28 Greville Street,
London EC1N 8SU
0117 971 1177
(for a list of three independent advisers in your area)

Institute of Financial Planning
Whitefriars Centre,
Lewins Mead,
Bristol BS1 2NT
0117 930 4434

TAX AND ACCOUNTANCY

Adjudicator's Office,
3rd Floor,
Haymarket House,
28 Haymarket,
London SW1Y 4SP.
0171 930 2292

Capital Taxes Office
Ferrers House
PO Box 38,
Castle Meadow Road,
Nottingham NG2 1BB
0115 974 2424

Capital Taxes Office,
16 Picardy Place,
Edinburgh EH1 3NB
0131 556 8511

Capital Taxes Office,
Dorchester House,
52–58 Great Victoria Street,
Belfast BT2 7BB
01232 315556

Chartered Association of Certified Accountants (CACA)
29 Lincoln's Inn Fields,
London WC2A 3EE
0171 242 6855

Inland Revenue
Somerset House,
London WC2R 1LB
0171 438 6420
(or look in the phone book for your local tax office)

Institute of Chartered Accountants in England and Wales (ICAEW)
Chartered Accountants Hall,
PO Box 433, Moorgate Place,
London EC2P 2BJ
0171 920 8100

Institute of Chartered Accountants in Scotland (ICAS)
27 Queen Street,
Edinburgh EH2 1LA
0131 225 5673

TaxAid
342 Kilburn High Road,
London NW6 2QJ
0171 624 3768 (9am–11am)
(for free tax advice)

INSURANCE

Association of British Insurers (ABI)
51 Gresham Street,
London EC2V 7HQ
0171 600 3333

British Investment Insurance Brokers Association (BIIBA)
14 Bevis Marks,
London EC3A 7NT
0171 623 9043

Insurance Brokers Registration Council (IBRC)
63 St Mary Axe,
London EC3A 8NB
0171 621 1061

Insurance Ombudsman Bureau
City Gate One, 135 Park Street,
London SE1 9EA
0171 928 4488

LAW

Law Society
113 Chancery Lane,
London WC2A 1PL
0171 242 1222

Law Society of Scotland
26 Drumsheugh Gardens,
Edinburgh EH3 7YR
0131 226 7411

Legal Services Ombudsman
22 Oxford Court,
Oxford Street,
Manchester M2 3WQ
0161 236 9532

Office for the Supervision of Solicitors
Victoria Court, 8 Dormer Place,
Leamington Spa,
Warwickshire CV32 5AE
01926 820082

CONSUMER AFFAIRS

Citizens Advice Bureau (CAB)
Myddleton House,
115–123 Pentonville Road,
London N1 9LZ
0171 833 2181 (or Yellow Pages)

Consumers' Association
2 Marylebone Road,
London NW1 4DF
0171 830 6000

Help the Aged
St James's Walk,
London EC1R 0BE
0171 253 0253

Money Advice Association
1st Floor, Gresham House,
24 Holborn Viaduct,
London EC1A 2BN
0171 236 3566

National Debtline
318 Summer Lane,
Birmingham B19 3RL
0121 359 8501

National Gas Consumers Council
6th Floor, Abford House,
15 Wilton Road,
London SW1V 1LT
0171 931 0977

Office of Electricity Regulation (OFFER)
Hagley House,
Hagley Road,
Edgbaston B16 8QG
0121 456 2100

Office of Fair Trading (OFT)
Field House,
15–25 Bream's Buildings,
London EC4A 1PR
0345 224499

Office of Gas Supply (OFGAS)
130 Wilton Road,
London SW1V 1LQ
0171 828 0898

Office of Telecommunications Services (OFTEL)
Export House,
50 Ludgate Hill,
London EC4M 7JJ
0171 822 1650

Office of Water Services (OFWAT)
Centre City Tower,
7 Hill Street,
Birmingham B5 4UA
0121 625 1300

Trading Standards Coordinating Body
PO Box 6, Fell Road,
Croydon
CR9 1LG
0181 688 1996
(or look in the phone book for your local office)

BENEFITS

Age Concern
Astral House,
1268 London Road,
London SW16 4ER
0181 679 8000
(or look in the phone book for your local office)

Benefits Agency
For advice on most social security benefits look for your local office in the phone book under Benefits Agency or Social Security

Disability Benefits
The Benefit Enquiry Line is open for people with disabilities and their carers
0800 882200

National Association for Widows
54–57 Allison Street,
Digbeth,
Birmingham B5 5TH
0121 643 8348

Office of Social Security Commissioners
83–86 Farringdon Street,
London EC4A 1PR
0171 353 5145

CHARITY

Charities Aid Foundation (CAF)
Kings Hill,
West Malling,
Kent ME19 4TA.
01732 520000

Index